Restorative
Grief

PRAISE FOR *RESTORATIVE GRIEF*

"In my line of work, I have seen a lot of pain and human suffering. I would say that Mandy gives us a "peek behind the curtain" of grief, but in truth, she rips the weighted fabric down completely. She boldly walks into places society has hidden away, holding space for us to explore our own truths in our own way. Mandy's writings make the perfect companion in grief. Her raw vulnerability provides us a roadmap on how to be introspective, honest, and gracious with ourselves."

Jessica Murrey

International Peacebuilder, Speaker & CEO

"'Restorative Grief' is a treasure; beautifully written, sincere, and thought-provoking. Mandy's journey through discomfort and pain, grace and healing feels vital for the times we live in."

Ryan Pfeil

Editor of Restorative Grief, reporter and writer

"For those of us in the throes of 'one day at a time,' this book is a light unto our feet. The bite sized daily readings are a balm for the overwhelmed and information overloaded soul. The 'for today' sections bring focus in the midst of upheaval. Mandy Capehart's voice is clear and gracious, leading her readers to hope through empathy and wisdom."

Laura Fox

Writer and griever

"The permission to treat grief as love was revelatory for me and my process. I'm so grateful for the safety and kindness built into this work and cultivated by Mandy. Everyone could use a generous dose of this in their lives."

Nina Pepin
Administrator, The Restorative Grief Project

"Mandy Capehart accomplishes something difficult by balancing the information needed to learn HOW to process loss with the emotional empathy needed to explore the WHY and pain of moving through grief. Each section is tailored to provide opportunity to move at one's pace, free of judgment or pressure that too often comes with such conversations. I learned I have so much work to do in understanding and restoring my life through a conversation with my grief and loss. Difficult? Yes. And now, much more possible."

Thomas Perkins
M.A. Counseling

"People want to be present with their grieving friends and family but aren't always sure how. This is such a sad reality when you consider how social support can reduce the emotional toll of grief. It helps people to feel loved and cared for; to feel less alone. Mandy has personally helped me to not feel intimidated to offer this support. Until now, I always felt I might do more harm than good because I lacked the appropriate tools. Thank you Mandy, for teaching us to mourn with those who mourn in a restorative, loving manner."

Heather Converse
Owner, Tree of Life Consulting

A *memoir* and *31-day guidebook*

Restorative
Grief

EMBRACING OUR LOSSES
WITHOUT LOSING OURSELVES

MANDY CAPEHART
Founder of The Restorative Grief Project

This book is not intended as a substitution for the medical recommendations of physicians, mental health professionals, or other health care providers. Rather, it is intended as an auxiliary support in conjunction with medical professionals in the pursuit of wholeness, healing, and restoration. Please carefully consider the ideas presented and seek the care of a qualified professional as you heal. Do not use this book in place of medical support or therapeutic treatment.

Special thanks to Ryan Pfeil for editing and to
Josh Capehart for layout, formatting, and interior artwork.

Cover image from Victor Freitas via Pexels

Fonts used: Anaktoria, Lato, and Times New Roman
Scriptural quotes from The New Living Translation, The Message, The New International Version, and The Passion Translation.

ISBN: 9798507206056

Imprint: Independently published

For you, Mom.

Thank you for showing me how to soften, surrender, and accept grace in the worst moments of my life.

CONTENTS

FOREWARD

Grief: A little word that stirs so many feelings in the depth of my being. Grief was something I tiptoed around feeling or even talking about until I realized the value of leaning into and welcoming it — not as an unwanted intruder, but a wise guide leading my heart back toward wholeness.

I can thank my dear friend Mandy for much of the shift in my perspective. The journey she has taken to embrace her story, her grief, and her triumphs has led me to face the places I have long ignored. She comes alongside with tenderness, empathy, and openness to the questions stirred by grief. Whether you have faced the devastating loss of a close loved one or are battling the weight of an unexpected disappointment, this book is for you. Each chapter and daily reflection will lead you with guidance, encouragement, and practical tools. As I read this, there were so many moments that my heart and mind encountered the healing presence and comfort of the Holy Spirit. This book is a resource I will use personally, and with those I counsel and lead as a Pastor.

There is an invitation in this book to realize that embracing grief is a critical aspect of us living fully alive and being a whole and connected human. Will you join me?

Kate Rhoden, Pastor of Living Waters Rogue Valley

Prologue

The Invitation

From Isaiah 61: He gives us beauty for ashes, and garments of praise for our mourning.

Right now, the air outside is foggy and gray. On the wall inside, a painting features a woman bent low in worship, adorned in vibrant colors. The contrast between the painting and the atmosphere outside is complimented by Frederic Chopin's Nocturne in C Sharp playing in the background. Grief is a contrast – a gray space. Grief is holy ground.

I write this introduction in the beginning days of the 2020 pandemic quarantine; the first of my lifetime and hopefully, what will be the last. As I observe the global reactions to the pandemic, I see the manifestation of grief is being overlooked by many. It is no surprise that our grief is going untended. Recognizing grief requires so much of our attention that we just cannot offer as we are struggling as individuals and world citizens to simply maintain some semblance of normalcy.

And yet, I argue that grief is the only "normal" thing we can expect in the middle of such horrendous circumstances. For those among us who have lost a loved one to this plague, we grieve together. The rest of us are cycling through varying levels of anxiety, fear, sorrow, and rage. The tension is real, and so is the grief. This is my book, but I will share my own stories only briefly, as I believe any healing you encounter here will come from your own story becoming flesh in front of you.

My hope in producing this work is to allow for the stories of loss to rise, take shape, gain acknowledgment, and allow us as individuals and a culture to transform into a new thing. **This is tread-lightly, move-slowly work.** Give yourself space to exhale, cry, mourn, feel, and float between steps as needed to receive healing. We have been offered beauty for ashes, but only receive the gifts we accept.

Whether you are actively grieving a loss, working through heartbreak from a previous loss, or simply curious about how to support yourself or others with more empathy, this work is for you. It is intended to create compassionate pathways through familiar storylines and give us better tools to love and hold one another gently.

After years of working through grief privately, I chose to pursue a career supporting grievers both as a writer and as a coach. Coaching is different from counseling, so I want to take a moment to clarify. Counseling is crucial for many grievers. It is reflective work, led by a trained professional who will help diagnose and analyze past experiences or behaviors. Sessions are usually consistent for a long duration, or until the client feels settled in their current season. On the other hand, coaching is a less frequent, forward-thinking process in which the client identifies areas with opportunity for growth. I invite coaching clients to lean into failure with curiosity. As each client recognizes where they would like support, a coach helps provide a specific methodology and framework to reach the client-informed goals. A counselor can function as a coach, but a coach should not function in a therapeutic manner without the proper licensing.

In grief work, we know the connective tissue between each client and their pain is always love. When the source of our grief stems from abuse, trauma, or violent loss,* it is the broken promise of love that hurts the most and takes priority. Grief is love, whether the person we lost is another or part of ourselves. As you move through this book, move with the idea that you are beloved (even if you are struggling to believe it right now).

*Note: If you are managing grief from an abusive or violent circumstance, please know this book will serve as a resource but cannot be the sole place you gain support. Coaching in all forms is meant as a subsequent tool alongside or after counseling.

False Narratives

Whether we are walking through a fresh loss or one decades old, we all experience the same fear of exposure when discussing grief in communities. Our Western culture struggles to engage the complex, nuanced emotions of grief. Even momentarily allowing discomfort to exist is intimidating. But in the constant pursuit of comfort, we have set aside our emotions, lost sight of how to hold space for one another, and forgotten how to mourn with those who mourn. Have you ever heard someone equate vulnerability with evil? I have, and nothing could be further from the truth.

As much as possible, allow the stories and resources here to guide you to a deeper understanding of who you are and who God is to you amid sorrow. My beliefs have grown over the years, informing both my personal faith and the way I honor grievers in my work. This book is as much a memoir of my own healing as it is a guidebook. I want to inform you that I do carry a grounded faith in Jesus. Yet even with my own strong beliefs, I felt wholly misunderstood as a grieving Christian. The church (as an entity) does not appear to serve grievers well beyond the initial loss. Much could be said, but rather than turn my work into a tirade, I offer my hope and intention that the story of my process will introduce freedom for your own.

You should also know I do not believe God causes our loved ones to die to teach us a lesson. The Old Testament is full of moments in history where this would seem otherwise, but the context of a historical work is never to be drawn straight into the present for application. God's character is consistent; He is constantly redeeming and drawing all of humanity back into His presence and closer to His heart. Salvation means healing. Death and loss of all forms are outside of His promise to us, as well as outside of His plan to remain with us.

I want us to meet the man Jesus, who in His time on earth embodied the fullness of joy and the lowest point of grief. He is the happiest person to ever walk the planet, and still we know Him as the Man of Sorrows. His demonstration of the paradoxical life, able to navigate gracefully through all experiences, is our North Star for healthy movement toward wholeness.

The purpose of including scriptures is not to simply use the Bible as a confirmation, but to express the validity of your grief process (as well as your emotional responses) as seen and known by God. Does that mean you must share my beliefs to use this work? Surely not.

The idea that God needs a loved one to die before He can reach our heart stems from a need to understand and explain away the pain. We want to define the "why." Simplifying God's nature to something so intrusive and aggressive is like relating owning a dog to getting married. **One does not require the other.**

By adding scripture to grief, we can inadvertently deepen pain with platitudes and a lack of understanding. This is often where the church veers off-course, presenting hope without holding space for pain. However, if we approach the scriptures with empathy, attentiveness, and respect for others first, then we will see His happy heart for restoration in all things. It is here we will begin to relate to the stories of old in a way that no longer binds us but rather, sets us free to grieve as we see fit.

During my own process, I struggled with my faith. It wavered and for a time, I wondered if I should simply walk away. I could not reconcile some of the teachings and interpretations of Christianity with the reality of what I continued to experience. Much of this book is framed for those in the same boat – perhaps you are ready to give up your belief system because of the way some teachers have impressed spirituality as the answer to all your sorrows. The global church struggles to support grievers in a way that is individualized, sustainable, or helpful long term. This is not an attack, so please set aside the pitchforks. The truth is that all pastors are stretched to their limits with expectations on how and what to teach, and grief is not an easily received message. If we want to be the church, we have to learn how to grow and support one another authentically and in love with more than thoughts and prayers. There is much to disentangle.

Regardless of where you stand, I offer my experiences as just that – mine. This book is a memoir only insofar as the content requires for explanation. Each day, the tools offered will incorporate some of the Christian Bible as context, in addition to wisdom from experts in the field. Perhaps you will find the scriptures hopeful; perhaps distracting. Your faith tradition and history is likely different from my own, and that's perfectly normal. No matter how you initially respond, remember that you are a fully autonomous human with the ability to replace the name of God with whatever resonates with you. If you carry a belief system that differs from mine, I am grateful you are here and hope you choose to stay. There is value to be found in all systems, all structures, all stories, and all people.

As they say, "Chew the meat and spit out the bones." Find what serves and allow the rest to pass you by.

Observing Self

As we find ourselves drawing closer to our grief, we must offer ourselves the same compassion we would hope to receive. When we observe our emotional states, we can make a judgment to shut ourselves down (i.e. – disallow the emotion to resurface out of fear of appearing weak, unhealed, etc.). Alternatively, we can make the choice to become curious about the feelings as they arrive and practice patience with ourselves. Be sure to maintain a journal as you work through your grief process, no matter what the daily prompts suggest. Your journal and thoughts will become immeasurably valuable even as a dumping ground for heavy emotions you're not ready to unpack. And if you're not one who enjoys journaling, that's okay. You can learn to do something new.

When Lazarus was dying, Jesus knew full well that His words would raise His friend from the dead. He could have prevented it, yet chose to allow Lazarus to decompose for four days before He ordered the stone to be rolled away. In those days, we are given insight to the way Jesus mourned with His friends. To the way He showed up for them — intentionally and with compassion —allowing tears to stream down His face.

The validation of an emotional response as demonstrated by Jesus serves to remind us that we have emotions for a reason. When we mourn with those who mourn (despite our own knowledge or discomfort) we extend the mercy of God into the lives of the sorrowful. We acknowledge and hold space for our humanity.

Restoration

Researcher Brené Brown has given our generation one of the greatest gifts we could ever ask for with her fastidious research into shame, vulnerability, and courage. In her work, she uncovered a common indicator that a person's rise into strength is often marked by behavior she classified as living with a "strong back, soft front, and a wild heart." I discuss this concept specifically in chapter eight with regards to boundary setting and building a circle of support. But internally, a person living with a strong back, soft front, and wild heart is willing to stand alone because they know what is right and good. We belong to ourselves and while grief can disintegrate our sense of self into someone we hardly recognize, this principle of self-pursuit is an incredible way to come home to ourselves. Holding our process and story close, with intention and dedication, is how we can find our way through the mess.

We experience grief like a sneaker wave, attacking when life looks like a beach. To resurface requires one to simultaneously invite the wilderness and confusion, along with the tenderness of a heart ready for healing and a sturdy center to hold us through it all. But the methodology to become one ready to grapple with the waves varies wildly. We all want satisfaction, and some would have you believe they found an answer. Throughout my research, however, I found evidence that often the answer given by the well-intentioned confidant can inflict almost as much damage to a person's faith and sense of confidence as the initial floundering in grief.

There are no wrong ways to grieve. Are there unhealthy ways? Of course. Just as there are unhealthy ways to drop pounds or quit a job. We are a society insistent on finding the quickest way to process. With grief, that often means accepting the surface level answer, hoping for the least amount of pain. But as any trainer will tell you, transformation takes time. Grief can become a moment of ingrained trauma to which you never return but repeatedly experience. It can also be an opening to celebrate life and transform the very core of who we are into a more integrated, generous, and openhearted human.

No one ever said life would be easy, but for some reason, we reject the complex in a constant pursuit of ease and comfort. While it is hard, it can be so good.

Let's move slowly into the deep end and learn how to tread water instead of fearing that we will drown.

The Window of Tolerance

One way we can move slowly through this process is to learn about our "Window of Tolerance." In his work at the UCLA School of Medicine, clinical professor of psychiatry Dr. Dan Siegel developed this concept to help us recognize when we have less capacity for tension than usual.

For much of our lives, we are happily cruising through life with a wide open window of tolerance. This means we have higher capacity for complex thought, decision making, stressful situations, etc. But when trauma or stressors increase rapidly (like in grief), the window narrows. We are thrust into one of two different physiological states where we actively avoid, resist, fight, or reject incoming information.

This can look like so many different reactions, but to keep it simple, we'll talk about volcanoes and icebergs.

- Volcanoes erupt. They experience tremendous pressure, cause great fear in others, and if they were people, would likely wonder how much longer they could maintain self control before exploding and causing mass destruction.

- Icebergs are slow, quiet, and frozen in place. It takes decades to see any movement and when we do, it is microscopic. They do exactly what they've always done… which is not much.

Neither one of these states of being is ideal, but awareness around our own "window of tolerance" is not an opportunity to bring more judgment against our capacity. It is information we need to practice patience and honor ourselves with the time necessary to heal.

Finding Your Story

When my mother passed away, I spent one week with my family in an incredibly focused, emotionally frozen hurricane of productivity. I considered this silent fortitude as bravery, as if I were setting the example for how to carry on. I numbed myself with food, alcohol, and entertainment. I coped by ignoring my memories and wondered how long I could maintain stoicism without addressing the indescribable emptiness in my being - mind, body, and soul. It was pure survival for those seven days.

On day eight, as I flew home to my husband and daughter, I had a conversation with my heart. A turning point loomed as I sensed I could not continue to rely on my own strength for much longer. The decision to look at my grief meant allowing my heart to be held by God – not humans – and to allow His kindness and truth to invade the arena of my life that would rather shrivel and hide. I wanted to learn how to embrace loss as a part of life, without dismissing the importance of living or of processing my grief. I wanted to move forward with intention and responsibility for the life before me. I needed to find a way to pursue healing and to feel connected to my loss without minimizing my pain. Grief and life are two sides of the same coin; and we can only avoid grief in our story for so long.

My mother's death is not the first traumatic loss in my life and grief is not limited to a death. However, it was this season of grief when I finally allowed myself to recognize the power of holding space for my own heart through the sorrow, even if it meant crying in public. The normally self-assured, confident leader needed to find a new level of humility and honesty. **I became hell-bent and heaven-sent on welcoming a deeper version of myself to the surface.**

The transformational power of grief cannot be overstated. But as we are willing to observe the grief, we must be equally willing to allow our understanding of God's nature, character, and truth to be revealed through scripture in a new way. The world, the church, the well-intentioned advice givers; everyone will offer us platitudes, comfort foods, and flowers to try and quickly cheer us up (again, I am speaking broadly of "the church" as a global entity in this context). Although you may not identify as someone who shares my faith, there is still a truth that we have to embrace: **Humans do not know how to allow others the space they need to grieve, and organized religion is not helping us figure it out**.

In my healing process, I found God offering a new level of peace, which does not rely upon understanding but trust in His character. When we are ready (and only then), we can trust Him to excavate our buried treasures. We no longer need to drown in the details.

What this really harkens to is that on the whole, churches struggle to handle the ambiguous, unending occurrences of grief. This often includes identifying the source of our grief as the church itself. The business of carrying on is alive and well, and those who are "not transformed" during their weekly attendance must somehow be to blame for their lack of progress.

However, we simply know that grief is not a topic easily discussed in public. It is messy, unpredictable, and wholly uncontrollable. We grieve deeply and wildly, unaware of when triggers will cause our simmering pain to boil over. As you work through this book, pay attention to the voice in your mind that repeats phrases you've heard over your lifetime. Are you whispering platitudes to yourself? Are you comparing your loss to a much larger scale tragedy, and invalidating your process?

This topic is so hard. I know many of us are hurt by the church and carry deep wounds connected to rejection and beliefs. I want to believe the church has never intended to disenfranchise or minimize your loss; and yet, it does so often. Even if your faith tradition differs from mine, consider that we both have much to learn by remaining openhanded with our grief. Regardless of our backgrounds, we can learn to embrace Jesus as one who pursued the disenfranchised and embraced the marginalized. His approach to grief was simple, invitational, and clear. As we internalize and practice loving, gentle reminders of how to process loss with mercy and grace toward ourselves, we will become the grief supporters we think we already are.

On Grieving Well

As you work through these pages, allow your heart to become curious about the circular nature of grief. The work is broken into five days at a time, each examining what is traditionally known as a "step in the grief process" but only to help create an air of familiarity. We know very well that grief is not linear. The time it takes for one to move through a single day of this work will be the same amount of time another person moves through the entire book.

Additionally, feel free to jump around to a section that feels most like hope for the moment. This is meant to become a resource that is honest, approachable, inviting, and safe. This is not a book of answers, but a source of wisdom to explore the emotions of grief and the restoration process of moving through loss with grace and compassion, no matter the duration. While fertilizer in and of itself may stink, it's useful when we work it into the soil. Left on the surface, it will have minimal impact and eventually be washed away. Doing this work is going to feel messy! You will repeatedly get your hands dirty and feel like you're working through unending piles of fertilizer. You may wonder if any of it is going to make a difference. It is not the book itself, but your faithful willingness to return to the work, day after day, that will bring about healing. Your consistent commitment to your own heart and story is the crux of this work.

This material is designed to bring life to the place that feels the most like death. If you catch nothing else, believe this: Your life is meant to overflow! Everything you say, do, think, and feel impacts your own story and the people around you. Give yourself permission to bring life to your own grieving heart before you unintentionally bring a half-life to those you love.

So, name your loss. Feel the emotions. Learn to grieve as you learned to love – naturally, through example and deep connection – because grief and love are eternally intertwined.

One
Understanding Denial

Denial is misunderstood. This state of preferable reality (where we think we are simply pretending that nothing is wrong) is a place where our grief becomes tangible for the first time. This cannot be dismissed. The shock and numbness of loss, if not allowed to take shape, will resurface painfully and publicly. Denial is not step one of five; it is not the first thing we grow through and then shelve. It is a protective garment, allowing us a chance to pause, pace ourselves, and prevent confusion from taking over our entire lives.

You may begin to accept denial by attempting to validate a quick dismissal of it. Early in my own loss, I recognized my thoughts jumping to scriptures that "made sense" of the pain I felt. "There is a time to live, and a time to die," and so on. While there is wisdom here, there is also a lack of space held when we dive headlong into platitudes without allowing ourselves to experience grief first.

I find little comfort in reading Ecclesiastes at the front end of grief, other than to acknowledge that others before me have felt a similar gaping void in their lives. This material is not meant to provide answers, but rather to help you find clarity for yourself through the tension of sorrow. Allow these words to validate your experience. It is my fervent hope that you find a safe method of processing loss with God and with others, rather than trying to navigate the waters alone. Perhaps you will find a similar draw to read Ecclesiastes or other scriptures, searching for answers. Go slowly through whatever you read, and know that if words seem empty, they will again carry meaning as you work denial to your benefit.

A few days before my mom passed away, I sat against a pile of pillows in a mound of blankets, still shivering. I could not catch my breath, and I was out of tears. I knew her end was close but despite this head knowledge, I could not quite understand how to express the simultaneous beauty and tragedy coexisting in my heart at that moment. What I wrote as a response has been a source of great encouragement through her passing and every subsequent loss. May this brief poem offer a lasting sense of hope like a familiar scent, carrying memories and a smile to your face.

Standing here, at the edge of the bridge across the ages, I am undone. The vastness of the unending horizon sends wonder like goose bumps across my skin and my mind and my heart and my thoughts and my soul decry the darkness and yet still I step, embracing the quiet mystery as a light appears beneath my feet. This bridge sways, rocking with the wind and each step falling harder than the last. I know my hands will raise and I know my heart will sink into my stomach but I know that both will once again be centered, wholly brought to that same, mysteriously quiet place of peace, where I know your name, too.

Day One

Everything Is Meaningless

> *"And the hits just keep on coming."*
> Lt. Daniel Kaffee, A Few Good Men

What's the point? If all our hard work, gathered wisdom, and effort fall flat in the face of disaster, how can we continue to try? Why bother trying to heal when the pain keeps getting worse?

These are my true questions each time I face a new loss or trauma. Sometimes I laugh and say, "What next?" As I write these words, I am living through both a pandemic and a natural disaster, combined with losing my own job and the knowledge that my grandfather is moving into hospice. These unending hits lead to a hollow feeling of shock — the kinds of disbelief that steals your breath and makes breathing feel futile all at once. Shock and denial would have us wait with bated breath for someone to tell us we misunderstood. The loss is not real; the person is not gone.

Upon hearing my grandfather had passed, I laid in bed sobbing. My phone slipped from my grasp and the tears slipped down my face. My aunt and I shared our deep heartache, a few moments of laughter, and then neither of us could handle speaking. Our souls needed to wail.

In these moments, there is nothing worth pursuing more than the next breath. There are no resolutions; no answers. Without breath, we perish. In our highest moments of tension, we hold our breath.

The call with news of my grandfather's passing was expected years earlier. But the reality of his death left me shocked that even when things seemed terrible, they really could get worse.

Ecclesiastes 4:2-3
"So I concluded that the dead are better off than the living. But most fortunate of all are those who are not yet born. For they have not seen all the evil that is done under the sun."

Sometimes the pain of loss leads us to rationalize how simple death must feel. The complexity of living becomes convoluted when grief enters, making even the simplest tasks seem impossible. Anxiety is the opposite of hope; and on this day, you deserve to maintain at least one small connection to hope.

For today

Practice breathing and exhaling. Really practice. Try different methods of breathing; both in and out of your nose, or alternating nostrils. In your nose and out your mouth. Breathe in deeply and like a lion, open your mouth wide and let your tongue hang, growling on the exhale. Force your lungs to empty and hold it for a few moments at the bottom of the breath. There are a number of resources about breath in the back of the book if you need ideas! Your breath is your super power.

Allow yourself to restore attention to the very involuntary habit of breathing. In moments of panic, shallow breathing and taking in more oxygen than necessary increases our anxiety to the point of helplessness. Reclaim your breath and fully exhale as often as you can. There is nothing more to work toward today. This is a task of utmost importance.

Day Two
Survival Mode Serves

"Survival mode is supposed to be a phase that helps save your life. It is not meant to be how you live."
Michele Rosenthal

In response to grief, it is perfectly normal to struggle with focus on daily tasks like reading or eating. You may reread the same sentence multiple times without comprehension. You may lose your appetite. Perhaps you will no longer want to engage seemingly simple parts of your life. This is perfectly okay, and quite necessary.

Survival mode can feel like another slow death, but it's more of a safety net for your brain. In grief, the confusion and fogginess of the loss turns everything around us into this otherworldly experience. In the week after my mom died, I remained emotionally detached from all decision making. If I needed to eat, I did so out of obligation to my body, not my hunger. I carried books around with the idea that I would read for distraction, but my thoughts could not remain on the page for more than a moment. Instead, the books served as a buffer between me and the people trying to talk to me. I wondered if this dry, desert-like state of being could remain for a very long time, as it seemed preferable to believing my new reality. In fact, I wasn't sure if I wanted to return to life without my mom in the world.

We know we are not meant to live this way, but without this crucial aspect of denial, we will also miss out on the mental rest our body uses to guide us through trauma. Sometimes it lasts a week;

sometimes much longer. Regardless of the duration, the simple act of allowing yourself to only survive to the next day is a great kindness you deserve.

Ecclesiastes 2: 1 – 2

"I said to myself, 'Come on, let's try pleasure. Let's look for the 'good things' in life.' But I found that this, too, was meaningless. So, I said, 'Laughter is silly. What good does it do to seek pleasure?'"

We know the great pleasure that comes from laughter for laughter's sake. But in the height of denial, laughter may seem frivolous or worse, disrespectful. It is okay to feel that way, and normal to experience shame at the thought of enjoying something in the face of loss. But we want to find a way to move away from shame as a teacher during our grief.

For today

We are going to embrace the beauty of a mantra. Choose a short phrase that feels calm, quiet, and brings a smile to your face. It could be a single word or a quote you've always loved. Write it down and carry the paper by hand with you, all day. Truly — carry it. The awkward beauty of forcing yourself to hold this phrase physically is the reminder of grace.

While it may be uncomfortable or somewhat disruptive, allowing our life to embrace discomfort and disruption in a small way (especially with something as lovely as a handpicked encouragement) builds confidence that we are doing a good thing, even as we are "just surviving." Surviving is a big deal, even if shame would make you believe you can or "should" be doing more. So, as you select your phrase, whatever you choose, let it be a reminder of the kindness and grace you deserve, no matter how heavy or critical you may feel.

Day Three
Mental Numbness

"Emotional states hold something important for us to learn in this process and should not be viewed as dysfunctional conditions to be extinguished or overcome."
Dr. Robert A. Neimeyer

By design, mental numbness (also known as shock) allows our brains to rest. The trauma of an act occurs once, but by our own thoughts, we repeatedly engage the emotions and heartache. This revisiting can cause the same physical reaction we had during the initial trauma. Regardless of whether we experience this retraumatization while dreaming or wide awake, the fact remains that without protective measures, our brain would overload with anxiety and full-blown panic attacks.

It is tempting to try and draw ourselves or other grievers out of a state of mental numbness by dismissing their pain. If we can distract or minimize the panic through activities, we think we will feel more like ourselves before the loss. But numbness will remain even in the presence of "happy distractions," because our body and mind are working through complexities they cannot logically understand.

During the first few months after my mom's death, I experienced true insomnia for the first time. I would awake from panic dreams with tear soaked pillows, unable to rest. Despite knowing I would be exhausted and mentally numb the following day, I could not fall asleep. Insomnia is a common side effect for those in trauma, and in my own experience, it is hard to tell which is worse – the running thoughts that keep one awake, or the disruptive night terrors that leave one exhausted. Eventually, I realized I was avoiding all thoughts of my loss during the day. My brain needed a chance to process the emotions, and was doing so when my guard was down at night.

Finding a method to cope or process through grief can be the difference between a solid six hours of sleep and barely holding your eyes open throughout the day. And without sleep, the numbness moves from serving as a barrier and protection in shock, to a perpetual state of slipping further away from ourselves. While I still experience occasional insomnia, I now have an awareness of what causes sleeplessness for me, and how to manage it.

Ecclesiastes 3:11
"God has made everything beautiful for its own time. He has planted eternity in our heart, but even so, people cannot see the whole scope of God's work from beginning to end."

Psalm 4:8
"In peace [and with a tranquil heart] I will both lie down and sleep, for You alone, O Lord, make me dwell in safety and confident trust."

God has created our hearts to know and recognize His peace, but the anxiety of loss is a direct enemy to hope. As we investigate our own anxiety, we owe our minds and hearts the kindness of observation over judgment. The mental numbness we experience is a guard; a protection. Shock allows us to slow the spinning and over time, settle into trust.

For today

Grab a blanket and a pillow, as well as the mantra from yesterday's activity. You are going to lie down in a dark, quiet, and still place. If you can use the floor, please do. Otherwise, a bed or couch will suffice. Place the pillow behind your head and cover yourself in the blanket. Rest your hands on your stomach, overlapping, and observe your breath.

After a few moments, audibly speak the phrase from yesterday's card. This is an exercise in meditation and pleasure! Remain and repeat this as long as desired until you feel something give. Like holding a good yoga pose, eventually you will experience a shift and release.

Regardless of what we are experiencing in the world around us, our peace is always a worthwhile pursuit. We can find rest through small moments like this by engaging our breath and giving our body stillness.

Day Four
Relief, Elation, and Grace

"Every broken heart has screamed at one time or another:
Why can't you see who I truly am?"
Shannon L. Alder

In your grief, what you may find beyond the constant cycling through each "step" of grief is that you experience emotions that may seem inappropriate for the moment. Feelings of relief or elation are complex but completely normal (even important) in early grief. Before we can wrestle with the rest of the sorrow, we must permit these less than welcome feelings to have their own chance to breathe.

Earlier I mentioned my grandfather passed away while during the writing of this book. He had been unwell for quite some time, living in a facility somewhat far away from most of the family. I wasn't happy to see him go, but was relieved when he finally passed.

While it may sound a little heartless, the relief I experienced with his passing is as complicated as grief itself. Reconciling my love for him with the freedom that came with his death meant struggling through the emotional thesaurus without leaving myself a bloodied mess.

This is where we welcome grace to the table: The place where we want to criticize ourselves or others for not responding in the way we expect. Denial is a gift, allowing our psyche time to move slowly through the emotions. And even more so, grace in denial allows us to see our own hearts as valuable — as valid in its reaction to the loss, crazed or sane as it may feel. Grace brings the blanket and the cocoa;

denial leaves us in front of the fireplace with freedom to daydream and find solid ground before standing again.

Ecclesiastes 4:6
"And yet, 'Better to have one handful with quietness than two handfuls with hard work and chasing the wind.'"

For today

You will make mistakes throughout this process of grief: Overindulging with coping mechanisms, snapping at loved ones, or missing appointments. But your heart is still with you through every step. As such, your heart deserves to rest under a huge measure of quiet grace that may feel uncomfortable to accept. Inside us we carry bruised, heavy places needing freedom to heal.

Therefore, before you fall asleep tonight, reflect on your day. How did you treat yourself? What was the narrative you thought about throughout your story and choices? Did you practice kindness or patience toward yourself and your behaviors? What abuses were leveled from your head to your heart? Did you call yourself names or curse your emotions?

Consider these micro, almost fleeting moments of self-flagellation and give yourself the grace to apologize to your own heart. This is the time to savor the slow pace of healing and experience each emotion as it comes – the time to see your heart as it is, no matter the shape or current condition.

Day Five
The Great Slow Down

"It does indeed matter what we do, say, and even think. Everything counts; everything leaves an imprint in our minds."
Pema Chodron

Allowing moments of grace for ourselves through grief is the crucial act of kindness we need to survive the intensity and overwhelming need to move forward. Indeed, we will eventually move forward. But without first reading the map, a road trip of such magnitude will result in missed turns and flat tires. We do not need to suffer additional indignities simply for the sake of healing. Quite the opposite – our minds will allow us to heal more thoroughly if we can embrace the humble, steady pace of one thing at a time.

Focusing on the small things we can handle restores our sense of control and involvement over our own lives. Denial allows us to pace ourselves, to daydream, and protects our heart against the shame of moving slowly.

What looks like reverse may just be standing still. I struggle with stillness, but as I mentally and physically practice being still, I am learning patience with myself to process at my own pace. Every single time I learn of another life lost, another home burned, another illness diagnosed, I experience what I've come to call "The Great Slow Down."

In "The Great Slow Down," light moves faster while minutes seem trapped in molasses. Simple decisions, like what to eat next, can feel weighty and overly complicated. Even my next breath takes more energy than I can muster. But in this pacing, my own body is giving me permission to wait. To pause. To be still and resist the litany of decision making, criticisms, and damaging thought processes our culture tends to rely upon during grief.

It is the onslaught of questions from well-intentioned outsiders (and our own inner critic) that cultivates shame. Although they *usually* mean well, those leading questions make us internalize and "should" all over our decisions. Such as, "Now that the funeral is over, will you sell this house or continue to live here?" Or, "How come you haven't donated his clothing?"

In our own time, we will make these decisions. But we probably seem to be taking more time than others would believe necessary. But we have to move slowly. Part of surviving these initial waves of grief is to pace ourselves with mercy for ourselves in this new unknown. Our waiting will make the outside observers uncomfortable, but that's okay. This isn't their story – it's ours. And now we are learning first-hand about the cultural discomfort with loss enduring. We are watching others wield a misguided personal burden to fix what they see as broken. But before we rush to bandage our wounds, imagine what would happen if your wound had a chance to breathe.

Not sure what "the fixing" sounds like? Notice those who offer platitudes of cheer and stories of their own grieving process. This feeds the narrative of "move on" with expectations you have no obligation to carry. We want to disallow others from "shoulding" on our authentic process. "Shoulding" is an action-oriented method of how others (and our inner voice) give directional advice based on our expectations instead of reality. We see the growth of another and think, "Man, maybe I should sell the house now," despite knowing we could not bear to go through that process yet. We must come to a place of believing our denial and sorrow deserve the space to move slowly or simply stand still. After all, "Peace, be still!" is not a reminder, but a correction. Choosing to remain still is a holy posture.

Ecclesiastes 11:3
"When clouds are heavy, the rain comes down. Whether a tree falls north or south, it stays where it falls."

For today

In grief, it is not your job to brighten the day of another person, lest you unintentionally stomp on their sorrow. If you're not sure how to hold space without fixing or shoulding, try saying, "This sucks. I love you. I'm so sorry. I'm with you."

And these are the same words you should speak to your own heart! Every time your heart lurches with pain today, say the words above to yourself. Your heart needs to learn how to rebuild a connection to the swimming thoughts in your head, but taking it slow will allow you to build a bridge that remains trustworthy in the strongest of winds.

Two
Unmasking Anger

As the most recognizable of stages, anger manifests when our emotions are not yet sure how to express themselves. Anger is the person shouting at a grocery store clerk over speed of service, or the quickness to blame others for our poor behaviors. Although we recognize the angry response in others, recognizing the mask of anger over our own pain is easily more challenging.

Anger is a necessary part of the grieving process. At no point do I wish you to set it aside as invalid, dangerous, or too much. But as you explore anger in the context of grief, I do wish to demonstrate a method of understanding anger with a new perspective. By reframing anger as a yellow light rather than a stop sign, we can take the pacing and stillness from denial and give our hearts a chance to become curious about the rage welling inside of us.

We will not, however, give any credence to shame as anything more than a quick reminder to move into humility. Shame is a liar – and although we may feel shame for our outbursts or angry responses, we must do our best to demonstrate grace to ourselves through our grief. When we move into humility, we can remember that we are doing our very best with the very worst of circumstances.

I recently spent an evening with some dear friends but managed to verbally annihilate each of them because of my grief. By the end, I knew something was wrong and sent a quick text message before leaving the parking lot. I sent another when I got home. I left two voicemails, and by morning, felt so much remorse for my anger that I asked for forgiveness of all three in one fell swoop. Like a waterfall, each of them poured grace on my heart and recognized that my hurts were valid. It was not shame that shifted my anger, but humility. Choosing to reflect and apologize rather than validate, defend, or justify my angry responses because of grief invited reconciliation.

Moving from anger as an emotion to anger as a tool requires us to believe that anger is a secondary emotion. It never acts alone! Instead, anger functions as a mask over the true emotion we do not yet know how to process. In my case, anger was masquerading as mistrust. I recognized shame and allowed it to point to my behavior as out of character, but I chose to ask myself what happened without shame as the filter.

Rather than condemning myself for the mistreatments, I asked myself questions about my intention. It was then I recognized my responses as fear and mistrust. I was grieving and felt afraid and misunderstood in our conversation. I chose to respond with my anger instead of my heart. But once I recognized my reactions as untrusting, I was able to express myself without shouting down my loved ones. I also found a healthier path toward hope for a healthy future.

Anger serves as a yellow light. If we do not stop completely, but instead approach with caution, we will regain our ability to look curiously down the street for oncoming traffic. We do not need to freeze in fear, but even with anger, we progress carefully to discover what waits on the road ahead.

Day Six
The Rising Tide

"Anger is a wind that blows out the lamp of the mind."
Robert Green Ingersoll

In the classic 80's comedy "Clue," Madeline Kahn portrays Mrs. White, who fully embodies the rising tide of anger. After being revealed as a murderer by the butler, she can barely speak. She rambles on:

"Yes. Yes, I did it. I killed Ivette. I hated her... SO much... it, it, the feel- it... flames. Flames. Flames, on the side of my face. Breathing... breath. Heaving breaths."

If you've never seen this clip, look it up online! Her complete rage with Ivette (the partner in her husband's infidelity) drowns Mrs. White's ability to think clearly, articulate, or even prevent her murderous actions. She is utterly overcome and unable to function.

Anger in grief is a sneaker wave, no matter the context of the loss. We don't need to see the wind coming to know the impact of its presence. We feel it on our skin; observe it in the sails. But within the grief process, we often do not encounter anger (much like the wind) until it is right upon us, ready to whip around any ship in its path. It spins up a whirlwind of blame and shame, and before we know it, we are caught up in the emotions but recognize only growing anger at what may have caused the typhoon.

When anger rises, it is typically an indication that we believe we are ready to survive whatever comes next. While denial keeps us in motion with daydreams, coping mechanisms, and numbness, anger shoves us forward with accusations and suspicion.

We need a fall guy. And in many cases, there may be a specific person or event to blame. Blame feels like a floatation device, protecting us against drowning and helping to make sense of our loss without sinking beneath the crashing waves.

While blame is a common reaction to loss, it is rarely logical. Like a Venn diagram, grief can become so complex that no straight line remains. And since we will encounter anger at every junction, protecting our thoughts against self-blame and accusation of others is the first step to recognizing the truer emotions below the surface.

Psalms 6:6-7
"I am worn out from sobbing. All night I flood my bed with weeping, drenching it with my tears. My vision is blurred by grief; my eyes are worn out because of all my enemies."

For today
Focusing our mental space and sorrow on a targeted enemy will drain whatever little emotional reserves we have left – especially when the enemy we target is ourselves. Today, let's identify any areas where we are blaming ourselves for our loss. Laying blame does not release healing but blocks it. In our anger, we will miss the horizon if all we watch is the breaking waves at our feet.

While you may have played a part, there are many overlapping circles of responsibility in loss. Trace your hand on a sheet of paper. On each finger, write a word that describes your involvement in your loss – directly or indirectly – true or otherwise.

Spend some time investigating – are these words true? Is it easier to understand my loss if they're true? What changes if these blaming words are untrue? This exercise can give us some mental distance from the emotions and accusations as well. This is crucial to keep us from identifying with an emotional reaction or condemnation.

Having those accusations on paper instead of running through your mind will help you start to heal from the constant barrage attacking your thoughts as you try to process the pain. Give yourself some mercy through this exercise by remembering that grief is a winding path; it can be very easy to get lost down a side road.

Note: You may also find value in creating a complex Venn diagram, but certainly do not feel obligated.

Day Seven
Anger Un-management

"The growth process is a grief process. Be gentle."
Sasha P. Tozzi

We all deserve the freedom to lose our composure. We love to read the Psalms with a holy reverence, but conveniently forget they were written by a frolicking philanderer. They deserve awe – but they're also the very personal and passionate manifestations of a mind processing turmoil. The Psalms are messy, reckless, accusatory, and beautiful in their honesty – transformative in their confidence. What David knew was the value of freely expressing his heart to a God who already saw it all, no matter the cost of exposure. Your character, choices, or circumstances do not invalidate your emotional responses.

Imagine what your journaling practice would sound and feel like if you allowed your thoughts to simply hit the page with no filter? Imagine if we approached grief, even in our anger, with the same confidence. It was only recently that I realized my anger in an abusive situation was masking my grief. I felt defeated, angry, embarrassed, and stupid. I fell daily for the manipulative behavior, and beat myself up each night. I often wonder if my anger would have morphed and healed sooner had I recognized the grief attached.

I wanted our relationship to be something different than it was, and carried grief from both my broken expectations and mistreatment. But losing our composure means I must embrace the uncertainty;

will I still be myself after I break down? Can I trust the unknown outcome, where I hope to find clarity or peace after releasing these overwhelming emotions? Even today, I am still practicing the art of losing my composure in honor of my grief. It can take a lifetime.

The vulnerability of allowing yourself to mourn through anger is risky. But so is bottling up anger for the rest of your life, only to feel the pressure building with each memory. Which offers the better reward?

Psalms 10:17
"Lord, you know the hopes of the hopeless. Surely you will hear their cries and comfort them."

For today
This will be uncomfortable, but discomfort is where we find growth! When a dam breaks, will the barren land mock the dam's apparent weakness or rejoice with the sudden flood?

What could we gain from losing our composure? Today is the day to find out. I know many people who have trouble crying. When we fight to maintain our appearance and stifle our honest emotions, tears are the first thing to be blocked from expression.

With that in mind, find a pillow, press your face into it, and start yelling. Yell as long and as loud as you need to. If tears never come, that's okay. If tears are immediate, that's okay. Let's see what breaks loose when we finally open the bottle.

Day Eight
Lashing Out at God

"You don't need a before and after story. You need grace for the middle of your story." •
KJ Ramsey

Perhaps the freedom we need from grief is not to get through it, but to remain present in the process of it. Much of the frustration I have experienced in grief is the wholly unpredictable ebb and flow of sorrow. Every special event or even photographs can feel like a complete reset in the grieving process.

Let's return to the life of the psalmist, David. David knew the value of an authentic connection to God. Yet, in his anger, he consistently accused God of abandoning him, rejecting him, and leaving him to perish. *Have you felt this way in your grief?*

What would happen if you gave yourself the space to become unleashed; untethered from the niceties and expectations of behavioral norms? What if you allowed yourself to challenge the pain of the moment – to ask gigantic, angry, unanswerable questions?

We know Jesus is called the Man of Sorrows, but few have allowed themselves to meet this side of Jesus face to face. In our heartache, we feel so isolated that we fear the admission of pain will offend or dismiss the declarations of God's promises. But we forget that God consistently demonstrates excessive grace for us in the pit of our despair – He is not offended by our accusations, our questions, or our struggle to believe in His goodness. But it is very difficult to trust someone with our pain when we fail to recognize the similarities in our scars.

Whether or not you are familiar with the scriptures, may you find rest knowing that He is familiar with you and your sorrow. Throughout the Psalms and much of the Bible, you can read how people consistently weep and accuse God, and still are followed by the promise of rescue. God consistently invites His called people back into a two-way street of trust and confidence in His promises.

He does not leave us in the middle on our own. He is the God sitting in the eye of the storm, watching the winds swirl around you both, asking you to trust Him with your anger and heartache.

Psalms 94:17-19
"I cried out, 'I am slipping!' but your unfailing love, O Lord, supported me. Unless the Lord had helped me, I would soon have settled in the silence of the grave. When doubts filled my mind, your comfort gave me renewed hope and cheer."

For today

We need a lighthouse for our lament; a reminder that we are not floating through the maelstrom alone. Meditating on a song lyric or a small phrase, as we have already practiced, can center our thoughts on the present and allow us to express ourselves freely. But for this specific lamentation, I want to focus on remaining in the middle rather than racing for the safety of the shore.

I love the Latin phrase "Usquequo Domine." It simply means, "How long, Lord?" Spend some time today journaling about this phrase; research writers who've used it or artists who integrate this concept into their work. I often choose to listen to "Until These Tears Are Gone," by Young Oceans. Sit with one or the other all day – these are meditative, honest offerings that will invite your anger to become untethered from the typically rushed movement toward resolution. Say what you mean! He knows the depth of your sorrow – trust that God will never walk away because you were too harsh in your honesty.

Day Nine
Yearning for Structure

"To love a thing means wanting it to live."
Confucius

When I started becoming curious about my anger in grief, I recognized all the places where my loved one will now be missing from in the future. I was about six months pregnant when I told my grandfather, Papa, that he was about to be a great-grandfather. Although the vivid blueness of his eyes had faded over the years, still they sparkled with all the excitement a man suffering with dementia could muster. His enthusiasm brought me such hope that he would meet her. We lost him a month later, and I was beside myself with fury. I felt deeply betrayed by hope.

These unfair moments of sorrow can leave us wishing for a different outcome, even years later. Losing someone creates a vacancy and it is completely normal to mourn deeply over the loss of what will never be, now that they are gone. I want them back – but what I also want is *compassion and normalcy.*

One of my heaviest revelations through hours of yearning was recognizing my anger at those who were not a part of my grief process. The friend who did not know or would not learn how to hold space for me; the person who told me it was time to move on. I wanted a predictable structure for my pain. As relational humans, we rely upon our connection to others to reframe what is broken. Like Moses needed Aaron, others lift our arms when the weight becomes too much to bear alone. But in grief, it is all too easy for us to demand a support system from people who are simply not equipped to be there for us.

I remember when our mom told my sister and me that she was very sick. She'd known for a month, maybe two. She was sad, but so steady. My sister and I had the same reactions we always have – she started to cry and react; I became stoic and determined to strike first with action.

But Mom did not waver – just as she acted when Papa died a year prior. And somehow, as we broke down through the next four months, no matter the intensity of it, our mom managed to remain hopeful and present. She was much sicker than she let on, but even in her pain, she allowed us to process and exist with hope.

We are still reeling with her loss. We always will. There is no moving on, as love and grief do not actually require us to stop loving or grieving in order to heal. It is a misunderstanding of the structure and restructuring of life around grief that believes healing only comes when grief ends.

As we begin to realize that grief does not end (nor should it) we can learn how to move into healing with grace for ourselves in the restructuring. It is here that our memories of longing help us build a new path to follow, rather than derailing us back into wishing for the past.

It is here we can focus on love.

Psalms 22:24

"For he has not ignored or belittled the suffering of the needy. He has not turned his back on them but has listened to their cries for help."

For today

It is necessary to realize who can and who cannot hold space for you as you grieve. But doing so feels like another form of grief in and of itself. If you are still unsure who is available to you as you restructure your life and thoughts around your loss, make a list of two or three people who can do the following:

- Allow you to share without offering platitudes or stories of their own – grief hijacking is real.

- Ask questions about your loss without trying to fix or explain your sorrow.

- Sit with you while you cry and not try to make you laugh or distract you from feeling.

You may feel a pull to include many people out of obligation, desire, or even something you can't quite name. It is perfectly healthy to keep only a few people very close. Attempting to maintain too many intimate friendships is a recipe for disaster.

Day Ten
A Bridge to Connection

*"To actively grieve involves risk. We have to relinquish self-control
and let our emotions run their course."*
Hope Edelman

Through asking these big questions, we recognize who can hold
space for us despite the discomfort they will inevitably experience.
However, **we must also learn to hold space for ourselves.** The
coping mechanisms, emotional outbursts, avoidance, blame and
shame cycling: All of these are distractions brought out by anger.
While they serve in the short-term, they will leave us with a poor
bridge between our self before our loss and who we want to become
for self, others, and to God.

Finding a path between the great BEFORE and AFTER of our losses
begins with recognition of our anger as a poor conduit for growth –
assuming, you want to find growth at all. You may find it easier to
remain in your anger right now, and that's okay. Be gracious to
yourself! We all move through this process at our own pace.

But when you're ready, allow the hidden emotions to surface instead
of justifying your anger with a fear of what may come. It is in this
place that the mercy of God faithfully allows our tears to become
salve; our rest to become restorative. Insomnia, which often
dominates my sleep patterns in grief, becomes no more than a
memory when my head hits the pillow. Engaging my anger means

uncovering an invitation to gratitude; never for the loss, but for another chance to consider impermanence.

Our goal is to expand our lives around our grief by acknowledging it will remain. It will take on a new shape in our lives, allowing us to grow despite the hurt and learn new ways of carrying our loss. This generosity toward self expresses a belief that we can sincerely experience our grief without getting lost in it. It is the place where we become bigger versions of ourselves. Not better; not more holy or less sad – expanded.

Without our permission, our lives took a new shape. Reshaping is a slow burn. If we are brave enough, it can become a steady process. Our goal is to acknowledge the space we need without requiring a destination – this is reshaping without arrival. That lack of control understandably makes us angry – but how we respond to it can set us free.

Psalms 55:22
"So here's what I've learned through it all: Leave all your cares and anxieties at the feet of the Lord, and measureless grace will strengthen you."

Isaiah 53:3a
"He was despised and rejected by men, a man of deep sorrows who was no stranger to suffering and grief. We hid our faces from him in disgust and considered him a nobody, not worthy of respect."

For today

It's time to take a risk. God already knows the shape, sorrow, and emotions of our grief and our anger. Anger is the yellow light – but most treat it as a stop sign. Rather than staying angry at God or blaming Him for taking our person, let's get it out of our heads. **Take time today to write your letter of accusation to God.**

Or maybe it's someone else who keeps trying to *shape your grief on your behalf.* **Whomever the recipient, express the things you're afraid to say.** You cannot offend God with your broken heart – and you're not going to mail this letter.

Risk being seen and known by God. Don't worry about scriptures, stories, or sermons. Be honest with your heart and the shape it is in – because we can't bake a beautiful loaf of bread without giving the dough some attention and reforming first.

Three
Negotiating with Hope

The more time I spend considering hope, the more I understand the nature of grief. I've spent too long choking on lies that say grief and hope cannot coexist — that one is the enemy and partner of death; the other, our goal. But hope is not a goal, nor is it distant. Hope is the ever-present promise that we exist in a living, breathing, and growing space of absolute love. And grief is not the absence of hope; it is a perfectly normal step in the process of life that invites hope as our lifeline! The reason so many resist the emotional upheaval of grief is the false narrative that inadvertently ties loss to an enemy to be avoided or defeated.

I have come to embrace grief and sorrow as a familiar friend. Not one I'm thrilled to see, but one that I greet with a knowing smile; the one barely hiding my tears but willing to accept another chance to practice humility and an active, hope-filled love. Embracing grief may sound fatalistic and too heavy to consider hopeful, but through the practices lined out in this workbook, I understand now the value and strength gained from leaning hard into uncomfortable arenas.

Bargaining and attempting to reorder ourselves after loss is not so much a state of grief, as it is a constant undercurrent. When we consider the level of disorganization we experience in the wake of a loss, the immediate sense of overwhelm derails our logic. We hear ourselves begging, "Make it stop!" and fully believe that no one is listening. We fear we are losing our minds, and in the process, we stop processing.

Think of grief like an estate sale. An entire home full of trinkets, trash, and strangers is suddenly flooded with an overwhelming sense of anticipation and anxiety. What treasures will you find? How much money can I make selling that old piano? Will anyone notice me crying in the backroom? These loaded environments are the perfect starting point to negotiate with hope in your heart. As you begin to sort through the piles of linens and books, memories and tears, allow yourself to consider hope as both a shopping partner and the one on whom you can call for restoration as you wrestle.

Negotiating with hope has two meanings here. The first is that as we unpack each box, we will learn to maintain a focus on hope in our thoughts. We must become hope-filled negotiators! There are still boxes of paperwork, writings, and small items that belonged to my mom that I have yet to unpack. The avoidance isn't impairing to healing; it is just that I know the weight of the box is less than the weight of the emotions inside. I am still cultivating the hope I need to open the box in my own time. It is okay that I am experiencing great waves of sadness, even after all these years. Hope does not need my sadness to dissipate in order to exist.

The second meaning I intend is that as we negotiate and navigate the loss (whether it is a death, a failed relationship, or a missed expectation), we must remember that we are negotiating with hope itself. We are not arguing with or against an enemy that has taken our loved ones or opportunities; we are in direct connection to Love. Whether or not you believe in God is irrelevant here; Hope itself exists in all arenas, all religions, all atmospheres. Engaging with hope in grief removes the stigma of sorrow and instead, gives us beauty for ashes. It is in this place of embrace that we practice expanding ourselves around our present moment to grow and include that which serves our healing, leaving the rest behind.

Day Eleven
A Temporary Truce

"The walls we build around us to keep sadness out also
keeps out the joy."
Jim Rohn

Fast and shallow is often the shape of daily life; get what you need and move on to the next. But hope invites us to experience a life spent deeply and slowly. Our grief deserves the same approach. Bargaining allows us a temporary truce with the alleged source of our hurts. However, rather than treating bargaining as a door to pass through, we need to treat it as a tool we can access anytime we need a *reset with reality.*

We want reconciliation and restoration to what we once held close, so we make offerings to God as if that's all He is waiting for. I remember asking God to prioritize my prayers for my mom over prayers for financial respite. As if I could simply choose between the two.

But when we experience a death, the immediacy of disorganization in our thoughts is paramount. We need to reset at our own pace and without judgment. Indeed – it is okay that we are not okay, or that our healing process moves like molasses in winter.

The trouble with bargaining comes when we believe God is the source of our loss. The truce we pursue is like begging God to simply lift His thumb from our backs. But God is not the source of our sorrow. It is very easy to believe God takes people from us. The platitudes and misinterpretation of scriptures are shared repeatedly indicating as much. We listen to sermons about grief using the Bible out of context, and we believe that if God is in control of the world around us, surely He can stop everyone from dying.

How can I be expected to trust God if I am taught that He takes from me but is still good? Scripture tells me that the enemy is the one to steal, kill, and destroy, so why then is God also stealing, killing, and destroying my life? God cannot possibly be good. This is not a matter of His mysterious ways that I cannot comprehend. This is an outright attack on His character and kindness.

With this type of logic, we begin to see the breakdown in trust and understand why so many are locked into a cycle of denial and anger. I think this is why so many treat grieving as a quick Band-Aid removal so we can trust the simple happy parts of life (and faith) instead of experiencing the complicated nature of both.

Therefore, we avoid grieving deeply. To dive into the disorganization would be to allow our comprehension of God to become disorganized as well. As my own healing continues, I am consistently disentangling my grief, faith, and addiction to certainty. God is not afraid of being disorganized, questioned, or confused in our minds. He invites it and in His kindness, resets our thoughts on hope. This is the very purpose of lament.

Job 1:21
"He said, 'I came naked from my mother's womb, and I will be

naked when I leave. The Lord gave me what I had, and the Lord has taken it away. Praise the name of the Lord!'"

For today

Let's dismantle any misconceptions about Job! This allegorical account in the Old Testament is used as proof text that God will partner with an enemy to demonstrate the faithfulness of humans, despite our sorrow. The man lost everything and then some. The above line, usually taken from the context of the book, would have us comforted that even Job trusted God's goodness in the face of great loss - so too, can we! But it is this exact theology that results in absolute heartache. By the end, God corrects Job, who experiences an awakened hope and restored heart connection with God.

Job sought relief but missed the chance to gain revelation. We cannot spend our lives pursuing an alliance of safety and false promises. God wants to reset our hearts in hope, even in the middle of our tears. *Spend some time thinking about an area of sadness where God is denied access.* Do you have a wall up? Ask yourself if you are willing to restore God's access to your heart without caveats. What about an area in grief where you simply continue to resist hope? Grief and hope, like sorrow and joy, can exist in the same space. Let them in. Be reset.

Day Twelve

Intentional Lament

"Asking honest questions is a healthy part of lament."
Emily P. Freeman

The mental exercise of a healthy prayer life restores a right relationship between us and the God we've come to resent in our grief. As we move away from accusation toward God for the loss, we must figure out where we are standing on the other side. One stumbling block to a renewed foundation in hope comes with the admonition to, "Just pray about it!" or to "Give it up to Jesus!"

The problem with "pushing prayer" as the first and foremost way to heal is if we treat our approach to God as a negotiation. Prayer is too easily transformed out of the beauty of engagement with the heart, peace, and will of God and into a mediation table. As if you could convince Him to act how you want.

Instead, allow prayer to be the catalyst for realignment of your heart with hope. We cannot exist believing we will never encounter grief, loss, or troubles. We must know how to navigate them without experiencing repeated crises of faith. Knowing how to grieve is paramount for our humanity to survive a great loss. Otherwise, we shut down and call our stoicism strength instead of recognizing it could be stunted growth. We must learn to drop our armor.

The psalmists and writers of scripture knew how to ask intentional, pointed, and authentic questions without remaining in accusation.

The practice cultivated depth and connection with God – they wrote and cried out in honesty because they trusted God would avail Himself to their hearts and wounds. Through their wildest furies, they found composure.

Composure in and of itself isn't strength; it relies on a solid foundation to remain when the winds blow harder. The trust we can cultivate in God comes from rebuilding your connection to His promises through a right understanding of His character. Not the character represented by Job, but the truth of His word as demonstrated through the joy manifested in Jesus.

Do you picture Jesus as a stern, corrective teacher or as a happy and patient friend? I've known both. But I've come to understand the former is a version of me, attempting to force my heartache into submission so I can move forward. The latter? That's the real Jesus – kind and generous, foundationally secure in who we are and completely comfortable remaining near as I lose my composure to find it in Him.

Job 42:3-6
"I had only heard about you before, but now I have seen you with my own eyes. You said, 'Listen and I will speak! I have some questions for you, and you must answer them.' I take back everything I said, and I sit in dust and ashes to show my repentance.' You asked, 'Who is this that questions my wisdom with such ignorance?' It is I—and I was talking about things I knew nothing about, things far too wonderful for me."

For today

Job went on a journey in his grief! The same is true of the prophets, of Sarah, of Thomas the Doubter, and every one of us. We can be honest in our questions without becoming so entangled that we lose sight of the shore. The psalms give us a framework to present our sorrows in a way that does not break connection. This is how we parent and how we try to live as friends. Why should we relate any differently to ourselves in grief? Or any differently to God? Our faith and our sense of self-worth must be honored through the grief process. If we begin to destroy ourselves for losing our composure, believing half-truths, or minimizing our own pain, we lose the opportunity to see what the information our emotions are trying to convey.

Present in nearly every psalm is this: A prayer of lament, an honest complaint, a request of God, and an offering of confidence and worship.

Write your own psalm. It can be four sentences or four pages. But include every section, moving to the next only when the former is authentically you.

Alternatively, you can write a letter to yourself. Express the weight of your anger and sorrow; complain about what hurts. Ask yourself to engage differently. Give yourself the vote of confidence and encouragement you need to pursue what is beautiful and restorative.

Day Thirteen
Unpacking Weighty Baggage

"The flight from sorrow leads to the loss of hope."
Al Andrews

When someone I love leaves this plane of existence, I feel all the feelings. Relief, heartache, disappointment, gratitude. It's like my suitcase is thrown from the train and flies open on the pavement, scattering my emotions like paper in the wind. Imagine if my suitcase remained sealed on impact. I could gather my things and depart without incident or exposure. I might feel momentarily safer. But I would still have the responsibility of a very heavy bag.

Learning how not to expose my emotional baggage during the grieving process led to a tremendous amount of guilt in the beginning and derailed my healing. I felt guilt when sharing any new understanding simply because I knew it might be adding to another's sorrow instead of bringing hope. I felt guilt that I was not in the same place of grief anymore. I felt guilt for wanting to heal! My thinking became convoluted and filled with condemnation. How much more judgment could I execute on my own hurting heart?

They say the depth of your grief reflects the depth of your love. In some ways, I can see how this rings true. But for me, I felt guilt that I wasn't grieving long enough. How long is enough to show the depth of my love? How can we even ask such a question?

Clearly, guilt created a distorted way of thinking in my life. Comparison and judgment prevented me from opening my heart and exposing my emotions. I knew I needed a lighter burden – and by keeping my bags packed up tight, I am always ready to pull back and run at a moment's notice. We must learn how to lighten our loads without guilt in order to find the healing we deserve.

Much of my guilt came from the false belief that what I wanted was the ability to *move on.* **Grief healing is not about moving on but becoming curious without judgment so that we may grow around our grief, not over it.** We are all working through some level of grief, all the time. We move forward when we become curious, compassionate, and lighten the load.

Maybe you don't resonate with the guilt I've described, and that's okay. Perhaps you are dealing with a version of the distorted thinking described above. Either way, it is time to open the suitcase and name the emotions you are trying not to feel – creating mindfulness of your pain without judgment breaks the heaviness of guilt. And thankfully, we do not have to go through this unpacking alone.

2 Corinthians 12:9
"Each time he said, 'My grace is all you need. My power works best in weakness.' So now I am glad to boast about my weaknesses, so that the power of Christ can work through me."

For today

Becoming curious about our grief and guilt requires us to ask non-judgmental questions of ourselves to figure out what is triggering or holding us back from opening the proverbial suitcase and unpacking one item at a time.

Pretend you are about to leave for vacation to be quiet, alone, and sit with your grief. Write a packing list. If you were to travel lightly, with only that which you need to process your sorrow (guilt-free), what would you take with you? What would you leave behind? Be honest with yourself. Maybe you need to ask the Holy Spirit to illuminate the significance of each item. The "why" matters – understanding your reasons will bring you to a new level of self-compassion and love for others.

Day Fourteen
Coming Back to the Future

"Certainly she was losing consciousness of outer things. And as she lost consciousness of outer things… her mind kept throwing up from its depths, scenes, and names, and sayings, and memories and ideas, like a fountain spurting."
Virginia Woolf

I love Marty McFly for his loyalty and tenacity, but I relate so much more to Doc from the "Back to the Future" franchise. The moment Doc decides "the past" offers a better future for him than he can find by returning to the future still sends shockwaves through me each time I watch! He chose to remain behind, sacrificing the known "present" for an uncertain chance at a different life. When you're used to sorting through heavy loss, the idea that you could just escape to a new storyline is enchanting.

But we don't have access to a time machine (huge bummer). Living with a fear of our unknown futures can lead to dangerous thinking and a massive influx of emotional pain! But right now, we do have access to wisdom that allows us to look forward, come out of hiding, and find healing for the present.

Daydreaming and cycling backwards in grief are powerful coping mechanisms. I love a good daydream! Often, we bargain by imagining a new timeline of events and attempt to will them into being. But this habit, while creative, is a fleeting half-comfort layered within the myth of closure.

There are true benefits to daydreaming – but my favorite by far is the creativity. Studies have shown when given space, time, silence, and boredom, the creative brain awakens in a way that the constantly moving and busy brain simply cannot. In grief, we have a unique opportunity to daydream about a different future that can detach us from our current experience. But we also have a grace-laden opportunity to press toward something that will create real, tangible healing in our present and future.

Rather than imagine my life without my mom, as I write this book, I am imagining a future that includes this as a finished work. While she can't be with me in person, I dream about how hopeful it will feel to see my words bringing encouragement and tools to others in grief. And as I work, the kindness of God shows up like a salve to my wounds, reminding me that I am never alone when I pursue this work of reconnecting to self and others through grief. I must learn how to navigate my new reality to heal. And to do so, I find a way to allow my daydreaming narrative to transform into creative space by trusting His wisdom to guide me through the process.

Ecclesiastes 7:10
"Don't long for the 'good old days.' This is not wise."

For today

Before anything else, I want to alleviate the pressure. No one expects you to write a book in the wake of your loss. Instead, consider asking God where you can trust Him to reveal an opportunity for creativity – become quiet, still, and listen. This is where we get the chance to change the wanderings of our thoughts to a more hopeful outcome.

One way I like to process grief through creativity is to do the things I miss doing with my person. My mom loved to cook, so occasionally I'll have the capacity to create an intricate meal and allow myself to feel whatever comes along.

Remember, this is not a practice to gain closure, but to internally **negotiate** *for a more hopeful future – one that doesn't include the avoidance of memories or trigger items.* In this way, I can remember how it felt to share a kitchen and think of meals we made together, and dream of when I'll share such moments with my own daughter.

Practice leaning into the tender moments with compassion and hope for a future that will not always feel so heavy. The space you hold for yourself today will expand your capacity to handle the triggers and weight of tomorrow. What little thing of hope can you create today in honor of your person and your growth?

Day Fifteen
Regaining Responsibility

"I will not say: do not weep; for not all tears are evil."
J.R.R. Tolkien

The idea of grief as a cycle (as opposed to a stage-based, linear process) is a relatively new concept. Even as recently as the mid-90s, Hope Edelman's book titled "Motherless Daughters" featured interviews and stories discussing the non-linear experience as a revelation.

And indeed, it is a revelation to many every single day. Understanding of grief comes from true, personal interaction with loss. At that point, we can experience all five "stages" in a single day or even a single hour. One of the most recognizable circumstances where this occurs is known as a "foxhole conversion." Facing death, soldiers are often documented as cycling almost immediately through all the emotions of grief and specifically bargaining for their safety and survival. Some accept Jesus; others impermanence – but all face the reality of their mortality and start making promises – literally bargaining under the gun.

Most of us are not under such intense timelines to move through grief and as we've discussed, the shame of "shoulding" on our sorrow is dangerous. Instead, we can pace ourselves and move fluidly through each of the emotions. Here, we gain the empowering responsibility for our own grief. Not in a way where we accept blame for our loss; but the opposite. We accept responsibility for our choices to lean into healing, or not. By taking even a 1% responsibility for our reactions and emotions, we will recognize that this 1% of us is carrying hope and a willingness to act on our own behalf. We pursue healing through our own actions and desires, rather than through an outside influence demanding we "move on."

The most profound and honest way I have healed through grief is professional talk therapy. It is simply a tool in my toolbox I go back to consistently. During some seasons of life, counseling doesn't serve and I take time off. But often, I recognize my need for a professional because I am requiring my personal relationships to become the detached and empathetic sounding board I need, rather than remaining in a healthy friendship.

My counselor helps me to embrace wisdom, find hope in my present, and provides reminders of how to endure through pain. I can read scriptures all day long, but the insightful question from an impartial observer can help illuminate how the Holy Spirit is offering healing. A professional understands the value of my tears. Professionals also have the experience and ability to remain neutral without trying to fix or address their own discomfort. This is huge!

An aside: Pastors are great resources for interpreting the Bible, but the majority of pastors (and other church staff) are not mental health professionals. Don't expect them to fill that role.

I want my friendships to remain supportive and engaged with me, but when I constantly express huge emotion or simply need to cry, the ability of my friends to hold space for my grief dissipates and our relationship may suffer. Give yourself the gift of boundaries in grief by allowing your friends to be just that; you can correct them if they try to inappropriately cheer you up (more on that later) but really, they want to love you, be with you, and see you find healing.

James 1:5
"If you need wisdom, ask our generous God, and He will give it to you. He will not rebuke you for asking."

For today

Think back to the friend list we wrote on day nine. Has your relationship with any of those people shifted? Don't panic if you notice something seems off. Instead, journal your thoughts and be honest. It's okay if some of those friends are more distant, or if new names should move onto the list. We can navigate boundaries with others with grace and health by paying attention as needs change. This works goes into boundaries in depth later on – so if you are discouraged, stick with it.

Speaking of grace, offering it to ourselves in this season may look like contacting a professional for additional support. Don't skip over it. You may try a few counselors to find the right one. This is your process and you are the pilot; but we all need a navigator to help plot the course. Just remember that if/when the search for a good fit in a counselor becomes discouraging, it's worth the effort. Try not to judge yourself for the time it takes!

Four

Excavating Depression

Have you ever heard of The Unicorn? This CBS show is centered on a father of two girls, grieving the death of his wife one year prior. The supporting characters navigate different levels of their own discomfort, certain they know what he needs and that it is "time to move on." Sound familiar?

Still, I was hooked in the first five minutes of the pilot. After a year of freezer meals from the community winds down to the final dish, the main character begins to defrost as well. Recognizing his wife is really gone, he starts talking about his sorrow and expresses to his people that he is ready to start healing, but in his own way and timing. And he sets the boundary *before* inviting his friends into the healing process – crucial!

And that's the goal – to start healing. It may look like spending a year volunteering or scraping freezer burn from lasagna. For others, it must start with a memorial service and counseling. But moving on? That is never our point.

Depression in grief is complicated and completely different for everyone. Anyone who has lived through it will tell you a different story of how it manifested for them. But what I continually encounter (both in and outside of the church) is the incredible dismissal of depression as a symptom of grief that deserves time, space, and respect. We want to move through it as fast as possible because it sucks, it hurts; it ruins our relationships, and derails our life plans. So we pray, petition, beg, and try all the quick fixes to find our way out of the basement.

Note: In this work, we are NOT discussing depressive disorders. Grief and depression are related, but ultimately very different situations that require very different treatment methods. In grief, we tend to remain connected to others and even feel moments of pleasure as we process our loss. Depression is beyond overwhelming, disconnects us from others, and frequently requires medical intervention or professional support. In fact, many grief professionals are now recommending support for depression from the beginning of our losses. There is no shame in asking for help and intervention, so if you know the extra attention will help, please seek it.

Hitting the proverbial bottom doesn't mean we never return, but the willingness to lament is really what moves us along our healing journey. Leaning into lament – this is where the good stuff comes out! The emotions that scare; the depths that bewilder. Please do not hear me saying that depression is a good thing – it can be dangerous and life threatening. But lament is a holy process. It is our manifested freedom; as we hit rock bottom, lament calls our gaze upward.

To feel the sorrow, grieve the loss, and mourn what is out of our reach; when we experience the depths, we can consider climbing again. But when we arrive in this place, we must be wary of the bootstrap theories, toxic positivity, and the self-aggrandizing idea that our experience will move the needle for all people. These ideas proclaim that we can remain surface level, read a few motivational books, and platitude our way to a better future – that we are the reason we fail or the reason we succeed.

But the truth is you will fail. You will see the light, the dark, and the in-between. You may move from being black and white in your thinking to find shades of gray, and then may even experience gray spaces becoming vibrant with color. I hope you will encounter pieces of your soul that you didn't know existed. In this place of lament, you may even become more honest with your heart, mind, and body than you ever thought possible. I can't tell you that it will be easy, fast, or consistent; but it will be worthwhile.

Experiencing depression in grief is the coalescing of all the steps, crashing into a heartbroken soul. Like the tidal wave that comes from nowhere, this is the season of settling into the dark night of your loss with a hope that believes a brighter sunrise will follow.

Day Sixteen
Becoming Withdrawn

"There's a darkness upon you that's flooded in light – and in the fine print, they tell you what's wrong and what's right."
The Avett Brothers

Distance is one of the first things I experience in grief. With each fresh loss, I find myself withdrawing to an emotional corner and waiting for the moment I can break apart. My vision becomes a vignette; the corners fading into darkness with only one thing in my direct path coming into focus. In part, I know this is out of avoidance of others – I don't want to hear platitudes or other false comforts. But after years of experiencing this moment, I now recognize this lowly place as where I can experience God bringing stillness to chaos.

Becoming withdrawn must be intentional. We owe it to ourselves to engage with the onslaught of emotion triggered in grief. Whether we feel sorrow or numbness, setting our intention to pull away from the noise of the world restores our authority over our circumstances.

We are not in control of our losses. And indeed, conventional wisdom would have us cut them and move on. To heal, I've chased gurus and guides up mountaintops and on retreats, but each time the multitude of worldly wisdom overshadows the stillness I crave in my soul. It is in this place of disconnect from self and God that I spend too much time focusing on the why, the unknowns, and dismissing the vision I need. In searching for the WHY of loss, we lose our focus.

The idea that we can trust God enough to draw closer amid great loss may seem laughable; even callous. When you have been raised in a culture that expressly tells you God is in control and responsible for your loss, as well as your salvation, what reason should you have to trust Him?

But God is sovereign – as different from control as dark is from light. His deep and intentional identification with grief is the very reason we can trust His wisdom and comfort. This takes more courage than I can muster most days. Becoming withdrawn into God in our sorrow means trusting that we can hide our hurts with Him. It means cultivating a soft front and pursuing tenderness.

Wisdom comes in many forms and from many messengers. Learning how to hold each nugget of wisdom against the character of God will help us begin to experience the healthy and joyful sides of recovering from loss. With patience and intention, we can learn to lean away from the guilt and toward the good. We are not after Band-Aids on bullet wounds; we want gut level excavation and groundbreaking discoveries of our strength in God.

Psalms 139:11-12
"I could ask the darkness to hide me and the light around me to become night— but even in darkness I cannot hide from you. To you the night shines as bright as day. Darkness and light are the same to you."

For today

Today I want you to lean into the idea of the vignette. Another way to think of this is as tunnel vision. While we typically try to include more than our own perspective, let's invite a few minutes of disordered, disheveled thinking today. If you are a mental processor, you can do this in your mind. Feel free to also draw a circle on paper, shading the exterior gray and focusing on the clear center of the page.

In our rush to move away from darkness, we tend to shame our thoughts or ideas into submission. We push so-called negative thoughts to the corner of our minds, right out of the field of vision. But for today, take five minutes to let your thoughts wander. Like popping the cork on our bottled emotions, let your thoughts and fears about grief come to the surface and escape without judgment. You can observe your thoughts without assigning "good" or "bad" to them.

As you withdraw into the thoughts you've been avoiding, consider if you can incorporate this little window of time into your daily routine. In grief, we tend to easily catastrophize all possibilities because of a fear of our unknown futures. Embracing those thoughts in a moment allows us to investigate whether or not the fears they invoke are true, real, and worthy of our attention. Are these larger-than-life fears likely to manifest? When we disarm the catastrophic overwhelm, our vision begins to widen again. We can see more clearly what is truly before us and what we need to look toward next.

Day Seventeen
Becoming Present

"We are waiting for our souls to catch up to our bodies."
Anonymous

Resting in the present may sound like torture. But we've tried to avoid it, and we still end up on this road even after dragging our feet. And we've tried sprinting away from it, but we cannot outrun the life we lead. Present is the only true option.

As we lean into this heart work, we are going to walk in circles at times, tripping over familiar roots and scraping our knees. Working to become present allows us to look at the path before us and begin to recognize the soil beneath our feet. We've walked this road before. We can again trip on the same root system, or we can notice our surroundings and learn to move with intention.

Running hard and fast toward healing will disconnect us from ourselves; mind, body, and soul. The quick pace is why we burn out in the process! The Holy Spirit is the incredible comforter of God who arrives amid our torment to fill our new and empty wineskins with a new creation; one that will sit and only improve with time. But just as wine cannot be rushed in the barrel, our own heart work requires diligent and present-minded attention. We must learn to accept transformation as it arrives instead of attempting to manipulate the process. Here, we practice patience with the present.

The grieving heart often sees stillness as stagnation or helplessness. I've succumbed to hours of nothingness in my own depression, trying to chase the ease and quiet I so crave. However, by hushing the inputs and placing my physical body in place of stillness, I steady my breath until my soul catches up with the constant rush of trying to heal on my own.

This is a practical method of fighting depression. How can we build a connection between our body and our soul in this season of loss? **By making the active choice to look at the ground where we stand.** We must find pacing in our movement to become present and use our time well. What arena of life have you avoided? Physical exercise? Dinner with friends? Church, volunteering? Family?

When I approach the edge of a cliff, I hesitate. This is good. I am making time to think, process, and prepare a plan. I engage my breath, deeply and with intention. The Holy Spirit is alongside you with insight, rest, and a revelation of the plan you need to find a way to cross. But you'll never hear the invitation if you're too busy leaping on your own.

Lamentations 3:25, 29
"The Lord is good to those who depend on him, to those who search for him. Let them lie face down in the dust, for there may be hope at last."

<u>For today</u>
Cultivating stillness in your body is challenging. When healing from grief, we need to allow our souls to catch up to our constant motion.

This is not a race or even a competition within us. We have all felt the disconnection between our body and our soul. This is our chance to engage and reunite the two in pursuit of healing from depression.

One strategy for stillness is practicing a "Welcoming Prayer", which comes from Contemplative Outreach, a network of spiritual individuals committed to the practice of contemplation. Simply put – notice how you feel in your body. Welcome the experience or pain, no matter what it is, as an act of consent for God to show up in your body. Speak your consent by stating, "I am willing to let go of this need for control or security, accepting this moment for what it is."

This practice, completed anytime you encounter frustration or sorrow, will begin to reset your grid for understanding the big, depressive emotions that arise in grief. Embrace your present moment. Your soul will catch up.

Day Eighteen
Becoming Empty

"Sleeping is the height of genius."
Soren Kierkegaard

I love rising early, but there have been many times in this season of grief when sleep seems far too elusive to willingly surrender a few extra minutes. The value of rest cannot be overstated, because rest is rebellion against the constant stream of input and noise. But even in grief, the cultural emphasis to move on and grow is counter to what we really need: Time.

Becoming empty takes time. Time is not the source of healing, but how we spend our time matters. In his book "Soul Rest," Curtis Zackery says this: "We can rest when we know it is up to Him to sustain us." To become empty, we must trust that in the space of stillness and quiet, we will not go without. Read that one more time: **We can rest when we know it is up to Him to sustain us.**

But before we dive into a monastic life, let's define empty in a way that serves the intent of the word and creates sustainability for us as a practice. It is not reasonable to drop everything and run away, just as it is not reasonable to memorize theories on grief. In mindfulness practices with the experts, you will learn the goal is never to empty your mind of all thought, but to simply allow thoughts to pass without condemnation, returning your focus to your breath as often as needed.

My tendency in grief is to search for meaning by inhaling anything that will distract me from my pain. Do I really gain something useful from everything I read? Or am I simply keeping my mind distracted?

To become empty, I must become still. My mind, body, and spirit all deserve rest. Grief feels like an attacking army, sneaking through the barricades and ambushing my thoughts at the worst possible moment. Rest is my weapon. Stillness of mind means disconnecting or silencing all the inputs and focusing on my breath as an intentional act.

One of the best ways I've found to get my daughter to sleep at night is the reminder that her body needs stillness to recover from the day and heal her injuries. She hates the growing pains, but when she remembers they make her body longer and stronger, she gives into rest. We know sleep is where we gain restoration for our body and mind, but the torment of trying to sleep through grief can make late nights scrolling on screens so appealing.

Can we find a way to simplify the onslaught during our waking hours to become empty and gain much? If we were designed by God to receive all we need from Him, then sometimes we must refrain from gathering all our own supplies. He is able and waiting to create a new thing in us, even in loss.

Matthew 9:17
"And no one puts new wine into old wineskins. For the old skins would burst from the pressure, spilling the wine and ruining the

skins. New wine is stored in new wineskins so that both are preserved."

For today

Only an empty vessel can be filled. Imagine a full glass of water being filled to overflow. Is that satisfying or overwhelming? If you're like me, the spill is now one more task to handle. Too much goodness is not sustainable – because saturation prevents absorption. It is time to make a list of all the inputs from which you receive "encouragement." People in your life, podcasts, books, events… be diligent to include them all.

Now, give yourself permission to silence most of these resources. They're not useless, but if the idea of listening or reading to one more source of "encouragement" increases anxiety or a sense of duty/loyalty, then you are only going to receive noise from those sources.

Becoming empty means releasing noise and making room for rest and deep, intentional breath. Where you may normally reach for a book, reach for completely empty lungs instead - and then refill them to capacity by inhaling through your nose. This can be where alternate nostril breathing becomes an accessible and quickly available tool (unless you're congested or sick).

To practice alternate nostril breathing:

Get comfortable! Exhale completely, then use your right thumb to close your right nostril. Each breath should be slow enough that you're feeling your diaphragm (belly) expand and not becoming dizzy or disoriented.

Inhale through your left nostril and then gently pinch your left nostril closed. Open the right nostril and exhale through this side. Inhale again through the right nostril and then close this nostril.

Open the left nostril and exhale through the left side.

This is one cycle. You will find better results from this practice with regular sessions, up to five minutes at a time. Balance matters: Always complete your breathing session by exhaling through the left nostril.

We must practice our breath work and exhale the cacophony of inputs because we are in a new season. The resources we've always held tight no longer serve. We need the new wineskin we've been promised. It is a mark of our genius to rest, breathe, exhale, and accept it as a gift.

Day Nineteen
Becoming Open

"When tears come… I am swimming in a hallowed stream…
My heart is at work. My soul is awake."
Mary Margaret Funk

The sitcom "Brooklyn Nine-Nine" is one of my favorite coping tools. I watch the reruns endlessly when I cannot sleep. There is a wonderful scene where two of the officers believe they are working their final case together. In an effort to remain strong, each holds long-range binoculars to hide their tears. It seems so useless, but I completely get it. I used to hide my tears. Behind yelling, behind insults – behind a book if I had one handy. I dismissed the power of vulnerability in a losing trade for my idea of composure. But no one can really hide their sorrow.

Every time I watch Disney/Pixar's "Inside Out", I sob. It is a perfect movie for catharsis. My stoicism is no match for the complexity of emotion made so approachable through this film. If you're not familiar, the main characters are five inner emotions of a little girl experiencing change and trauma. In her lust for a good life, Joy tries to control the others and prevent their little girl from experiencing any influence from Sadness. But while Joy and Sadness lead a dangerous adventure, the remaining emotions of Disgust, Anger, and Fear try to run the show, masquerading as Joy.

Spoiler: They do a terrible job. Soon, Joy and Sadness are reunited with their team, and the necessary balance of emotion is clear – some moments in life require a complex emotional response. In our grief, we are invited to become open to the possibility that a happy moment contains some sorrow, or that a frustrating moment holds hidden hope. Openness to a new understanding allows our souls to reject the lie of destruction. We are never hopeless.

In a depressive state, I can choose to engage the intrusive thoughts, hopelessness, and tears with disdain or with curiosity. Allowing myself to cry and become vulnerable connects me to God within me, through our shared revelation of how sadness and pure joy really can coexist. **Tears are a holy gift.** Each one is counted by God; each releases endorphins proven to dull physical pain. Tears engage your parasympathetic nervous system, allowing you to self-soothe. They brighten our moods, cool our brains, lower our stress, remove toxins, and connect us to community. Do the research. Tears heal our bodies.

John 11:35
"Jesus wept."

For today

When was the last time you allowed yourself to cry when you really would have preferred to hold back? The most joyful, loving, playful, and powerful Rabbi to walk the planet wept publicly – even with the knowledge that He would soon resurrect His friend. If Jesus frequently chose such a vulnerable act, why do I so often resist the same vulnerability? Because I need intention. I first need to establish a grounded point of connection to safely release my tears.

Earlier we worked on unleashing big emotions while moving specifically through anger. For now, we are going to learn about a practice known as "Centering Prayer." The goal of this silent method is to deepen our relationship to God, but also, to open our soul to stillness and invite hope to enter the picture once again. No need to practice crying! Our tears will come when they're ready. But our soul deserves the space to awaken to the beauty of vulnerability.

To begin, sit quietly and alone, eyes closed. Choose a word to symbolize your intention in this prayer time, both to God and your own actions.

This word will be your guidepost – focus on it the whole time. If your thoughts become intrusive in this sacred space, gently return your attention to your chosen word or phrase and find a small smile. Take as much or as little time as you need. Completed daily, this practice will cultivate stillness and a safe space within yourself to emote vulnerably and with daring, impossible hope.

Day Twenty
Becoming Honest

"When we cannot doubt in the presence of God, we will be forced to doubt elsewhere."
John Mark McMillian

I've yet to encounter a grieving soul who found lasting comfort or welcome in the church throughout their grief. The initial meal trains and outpouring of empathy are beautiful and honest, but just not sustainable. Indeed, most of us have no idea how to hold space for another person long term. One of the most damaging things I've witnessed in this context is the honest expression of doubt being met with a Bible verse about how grief and lament have an ending point.

The not-so-secret truth about the church? No one knows all the answers. But the dualistic mindset of modern-day religion prevents the discomfort needed to sit in the mystery and confusion of grief. In response, we too quickly break out the Bible and use every scripture we can to cheer those carrying loss. Many a well-meaning "encourager" has silenced the honest broken heart. "Rejoice always!" is a beautiful command, but in the depths of loss, being told what to do can cause greater disconnection. It usually has the opposite effect of the healing intended.

Becoming honest about the depth of grief we experience is exactly what God taught us to do through all of scripture. Earlier, we practiced becoming honest with God in our questions, but now is the time we become honest with ourselves.

When I experience depression, the last thing I want is to be self-reflective or thankful, yet a position of gratitude and honest connectivity is what pulls me out of my detachment and breaks fear. But I have to come to this conclusion in my own timing. I can't be commanded into confidence. Doubt is not a villain. Doubt is information that allows us to ask questions and become familiar with the unanswered prayer as a sign of wisdom greater than our own. Doubt is nothing to fear.

Admitting my own inability to trust God's goodness in the face of grief was terrifying. I hardly had the courage to say it aloud. Yet in that place of questioning arose a confidence that even in my sorrow, God will reveal a connection for me between His heart and mine. My doubt becomes the soil in which my roots grow deeper, even as winter settles in and the winds blow harder. Don't allow the desire to be correct, comforted by others, or secure in a community distract you from your direct access to God through your heart's most honest cries. After all, Thomas' doubt was met with an answer and direct invitation into greater intimacy. Jesus relieved his fears and doubts with a blessing of peace. Well worth the honesty.

John 20:26b-27
"'Peace be with you,' he said. Then he said to Thomas, 'Put your finger here, and look at my hands. Put your hand into the wound on my side. Don't be faithless any longer. Believe!'"

For (the end of) today
We are going to observe ourselves in this place of depression with an Ignatian practice called The Examen. There are five simple steps that

will hopefully draw some self-compassion and honest thanksgiving from our hearts. In the presence of God, honest thanksgiving embraces grief.

Ask God for sight and light. "I want to look at my day with God's eyes, not merely my own."

Practice gratitude. "The day I've just lived is a gift, no matter the content or outcomes. I am grateful for it."

Consider your day. "I will be guided by the Holy Spirit as I think carefully about the content of my day."

Embrace your shortcomings. "I accept what needs growth, grace, and correction in me and my life."

Look with hope toward tomorrow. "I invite you, God, to show me where I need you the most."

Five
Nonviolent Acceptance

Before we wade into the waters of acceptance, I want to remind you that we are not about finding a way to "move on." By processing our grief with God at our side, not through blame but partnership and consent, we can find moments of bravery. Courage comes from facing the dark night of the soul, rising with the sun, and stretching our heart toward heaven with gracious expectation and generous faith.

When we finally reach this "stage" of the grief process, we get to practice a liberal and curious understanding of faith as we explore the options ahead, make plans, and continue the complicated work of healing.

But acceptance can feel like a form of violence – both against us and our lost loved ones. The very idea of acceptance brings my cynical critic to the surface. Of course, I do not want to accept that

I've lost someone. It feels like a disservice to their memory to accept their passing. It is an emotional assault.

The finality of "accepting" the loss is genuinely a good place to arrive, but it is not the destination. Traditional models of grief have allowed acceptance to remain as the last step, but thankfully, we know better! As we demand better of a theory, we can engage better for our own heart work and growth.

It is important that we understand the difference between violent and nonviolent communication before we start applying the ideas of accepting loss and embracing a type of new normal. Violent communication is any communication toward others or self that would be a moralistic judgment or exert pressure to act a certain way. The idea that we can bully or condemn ourselves with "shoulding" and name calling is nothing new, but when considered in the framework of processing grief, violent communication is practically all we know. The most common way we encounter internal violent communication is through cognitive distortions such as labeling, emotional reasoning, catastrophizing, all-or-nothing thinking, and more.

We cannot manipulate ourselves into wholeness. In the pursuit of restorative grief, we owe ourselves the grace required to welcome wholeness with mercy, responsibility, and compassion. If we block compassion with aggressive assertions and bribery, we are attempting to fix that which is outside of our control. In our effort to understand on an intellectual level, we lean toward providing feedback, sympathy (instead of empathy), education, and consolation. These and more are half-truths that sound like comfort but fill the space with shame. It's like someone insisting that you can handle grief because grief is hard, and you can handle hard things.

Grief isn't "hard." It is complicated, confusing, and layered with emotions: Way beyond hard. Hard things are factual, rational, and surmountable. Hard looks like lifting tires and confronting sexism and writing a damn book. Don't be ashamed when your healing takes more time than writing a book. It can be as long lasting as love itself, but that does not mean our pain has to have the same weight through the entire process as well.

We can reshape our grief by treating ourselves with the loving, nonviolent communication offered through a restorative relationship with creation and the Creator. It will probably feel unnatural, but with practice, we will return to this habit of engaging our grief with less resistance; as a natural part of our human design. Put another way, we can embrace the inner refinement of our sharp edges, allowing a softened version of ourselves to hit the shore like sea glass.

Those bright treasures from the ocean are soothed and softened over time — not forcibly reshaped by a rock tumbler. The Man of Sorrows Himself embodies the paradox of joy and grief — the very nature of empathy. But before we dive into the beauty of restoration with Jesus, we must recognize the ways we have abused ourselves with a concept of moving on via acceptance.

Day Twenty One
Recognition

"Reality is always kinder than what I'm believing about it."
Byron Katie

Does healing seem unattainable to you? Even as we navigate on our own timeframe and through every level of grief, gathering the presence of mind to find acceptance might feel out of reach. But in this place, away from the noise of theories and well-meaning friends, we can embrace the idea of a new normal with grace.

Acceptance will not be the final accomplishment we hope for through studying our grief. However, the increase of our curiosity about our own emotional reactions will be an accomplishment worth celebrating! Recognizing grief, in all its sneaky forms, requires attentiveness and willingness to see with new sight and new ideas.

In this space of reorganization, we must recognize the way we have allowed our heart, mind, body, and soul to embrace secrecy from one another. Where have we become disjointed? Reconnecting all the arenas of our being allows God to teach us the nonviolent methods of cleaning out the suitcases after this long, arduous trip. And while the trip is never over, we can still rely on the truth of our circumstances with a clearer head and kinder words.

My gut reaction to grief is anger, nine times out of ten. From the position of anger, I am disconnected from my heart – my head reels with worst case scenarios, guilt trips, and accusations of what will go wrong next. Just as deadly are the moralistic judgments and self-denial of our connection to the loss.

Have you ever uttered something like these examples of dismissive statements to yourself or another? I have.

Did you really know her that well anyway?

You hadn't spoken with him in years.

I'm sorry, but this client doesn't know someone died. Get it together.

It's not like you were still married to her.

While some may suffer from the lack of social graces to say something this rude to you, think back if you've spoken this way to yourself as well. These **self-inflicted** wounds of violent communication prevent me from demonstrating the necessary empathy and honest self-expression that I need to move forward. It is up to us to evaluate our depth of connection and loss, no matter the circumstances.

Psalms 147:3
"He heals the brokenhearted and bandages their wounds."

For today

Reorganizing our life around loss is time consuming and detailed. We need empathy, not condemnation! On a blank page, draw two columns and title them "Violent" and "Nonviolent." Under "Violent", list the intrusive thoughts or words spoken to you (or by you) that sound like condemnation, judgment, or dismissal. Do they contain the word, "should"? Then include it here.

Before writing under the "Nonviolent" column, ask the Holy Spirit to show you a new response of empathy for each statement. Accept the excessive generosity of each response, even if you don't fully believe it. The comfort received from God is inexplicable and sometimes hard to accept for ourselves. But once we do, we are quicker to recognize and reject invalid, violent responses rather than hiding them away in our hearts.

Another way of uncovering the way we speak to ourselves is to investigate different types of cognitive distortions.* With a lens of compassion, ask yourself: Am I experiencing any of these patterns of thought? By identifying the cognitive distortions we may be experiencing, we can become more aware of how our brains drift away from the intentional work of healing. This is how we can begin believing better about ourselves, our future, and our hope for restoration.

*There is a link for more information about cognitive distortions in the resources section.

Day Twenty Two
Understanding New Normal

"I'll be seeing you in all the old familiar places that this heart of mine embraces, all day through."
Billie Holiday

Let's reject the idea that loss is okay. Loss is never okay. It's not okay that they died, but you are going to be okay. Earlier I mentioned the idea that deep grief is the proper response to deep love. But it's a little too simple for me. To risk great love is to risk great grief, but my love of my person doesn't subside or diminish simply because I've allowed the shape and intensity of my sorrow to shift.

Navigating with hope into our new normal requires us to embrace the nonviolent method of empathic communication. While I'm not an expert, I recognize the language used because it is familiar to me from participating in counseling for my own loss and trauma. In my experience, when we learn new skills and concepts, we tend to look for an unsuspecting person to practice upon. It makes me think about hearing a sermon and suddenly wishing my husband could be listening to the same talk. Not only is this making an assumption and judgment about his process, it's also not helpful – you cannot resuscitate a body without oxygen in your own lungs. We must figure out our new normal first before coming alongside others to find theirs.

Nonviolent communication begins with observing your own behaviors and identifying your feelings/bodily sensations. Make neutral statements about what you see or hear in yourself; no filters and no attempts to rationalize. Simply observe.

From there, ask yourself what you care about. What do you want? What will be included in your "new normal" that is important to you? Is there an emotional or physical need you would like to address right away? Finally, armed with this observational information about your status in life, name something practical that would fulfill a need right now.

Here, we are starting to reorganize our lives in our newness, as we too are now new with our loss. We admit our needs have changed. We are shifted. We are inviting new life. We are learning to breathe again.

2 Thessalonians 3:5
"May the Lord lead your hearts into a full understanding and expression of the love of God and the patient endurance that comes from Christ."

<u>For today</u>

If this exercise is too intense, step away and return another time. But I believe we can find grace for ourselves and practice nonviolent communication from the perspective of our loved ones. I know when I imagine the voice and advice I might receive from someone I've lost, it's always much kinder than I had been speaking to myself. That said, I also realize the relationship may have been quite complicated. With that in mind, imagine what you hope they would want for you, moving forward.

Let's invite our creative minds to get involved in our healing again. Pretend you are sitting with someone you've lost and admired. If you have not yet done so, observe your behavior and the sensations in your body. Make a neutral statement about what you see in yourself and continue the rest of the practice described above. Now, because you know and love the words of the person you lost, imagine how they would be looking at you in this moment. Allow your creative mind to imagine what they might say to you. The vulnerability required for this exercise will take time. Be patient – this is a great way to find hope in your loss. What I hope you will encounter is a little humor, a little movement — a reminder that you are doing an incredible job showing up for yourself.

If you are grieving a loss that did not begin with the death of a loved one, allow your creative mind to revisit a joyful memory around your loss. This may also be a time to return to a physical location associated with your loss and create new memories. Invite laughter – rewrite the script and invite hope back into your narrative! Remind your heart that joy is possible, even in the presence of grief. Your complexity as a human is a testament to your capacity to heal and grieve in the same breath. Exhale deeply and if you can, practice a few moments of gratitude for your breath and life today.

Day Twenty Three
Impermanence

"Nothing is more natural than grief, no emotion more common to our daily experience. It's an innate response to loss in a world where everything is impermanent."
Stephen Levine

Explaining loss to a child is really challenging. They are still learning about their own relationship to others in the world who simply live far away, let alone to those we've lost. As a young parent, I remember our daughter beginning to recognize that she and I were two separate people. Always shifting, we steadily find our identity as we grow, often through our connection to others. Slowly, she learned to reorder her attachment to me as an individual. As we grow in relationships, we all continue to cultivate healthy connections rooted by deep love and affection.

But when we lose someone with profound involvement in our lives, confusion reigns. We can easily intellectualize loss. We've read books; we have the misguided 5 steps memorized. But despite this head knowledge of loss, the heart is weighted with wild emotion. Sometimes I picture the heart itself literally being pulled lower with the heaviness of grief; drawn further away from the head. How can we accept the ephemeral nature of life, lighten our hearts, and strengthen the connection between head and heart? How do we build openhanded attachment?

Accepting the impermanence of life (and of our own lives) is a scary prospect. We fear death because we fear pain for ourselves and others. That may be an oversimplification, but if we want to remove the filter of fear, we must resolve our minds against the subtle violence of the victim mentality.

Have you ever declared the world is working against you? This prevents you from experiencing the real feelings and emotions weighing you down. If you continually express the perception of a world in attack mode, you will repeat the cycle of victimizing yourself and lack responsibility. We accuse and miss the opportunity to be still, reflecting on the truth of our short time on earth. We miss out on perfect love.

Embracing impermanence triggers deep joy. I am a devoted wine geek (and not to your mama's white zinfandel). Over the years of my wine education, the caliber and quality of the wines I've tasted astounds me. I have a deep gratitude for those who would share the stars of their cellars because like all things, I know this is likely a once in a lifetime opportunity to try some of these treasures. We sip slowly because this exact moment will never return. Imagine if we found delight in all moments with this same intentionality. When was the last time you savored your breath?

John 14:27
"I am leaving you with a gift - peace of mind and heart. And the peace I give is a gift the world cannot give. So don't be troubled or afraid."

For today

Create a ritual of impermanence. If you're not a wine lover like me, then your job is to identify something that makes you want to slow down. What thing in this life makes you want to slow down time and savor the moment? Take some time to figure out what you could bring into your home as a ritual for remembrance of our present lives and impermanent state. For our family, it is a good bottle of port and a chunk of sourdough bread.

As often as we can remember, my husband and I will hold space to take communion together. As apprentices of Jesus, we value the sacraments as a reminder that we are breathing and full of life because of His kindness. But as humans, a moment of focused intent like sharing communion brings our heart to the present.

If communion feels too intense, you can create another ceremonious slowdown that works for your life. To pursue delight in moments of connectedness allows us to feel connected to things we've allowed to numb in our hearts through grief and loss. Here, we welcome hope to spring.

Day Twenty Four
The Value of Discomfort

"Be full of sorrow, that you may become a hill of joy; weep, that you may break into laughter."

Rumi

There is a lot of talk about discomfort throughout this work, and for good reason. Very little is comforting in grief. Despite this truth, we fail to recognize the value of discomfort out of avoidance, fear, and dismissal of our true needs.

Allowing our deepest sorrows to take up space is not our idea of a great time. We crave warm fires without chopping wood, the prosperity without sacrifice, and the false comfort of platitudes to move away from our grief. We want to identify with happiness and pretend the rest is for someone else to understand. Yet we are hindered in our healing if all we pursue is comfort and a return to the simpler time. Grief deserves as much attention as joy or laughter, for often they are reliant upon one another.

Instead of avoiding discomfort, we must ask ourselves what we need. Be on guard against "should" language creeping in here to shame or strategize.

Hint: Asking what we need often looks like making a list or setting intentions. Controlling yourself with a list will not remove the discomfort or pain but will move you away from engaging with what you need to heal. It puts you into task mode instead of turning you toward simply existing.

What critical, intangible things in life do you need to be sustained or moved forward? These needs do not rely upon people, specific actions, or things you can acquire. They are found in the simplicity and quiet of reflection.

It is uncomfortable to be quiet. We want motion; action. Our ego desires accomplishment and progress. But we must learn to value discomfort as a tool with a purpose to carve and reshape our understanding of self and others. It is in this place of willing surrender that we become curious over judgmental, open over controlling, and grateful over laden with guilt.

How can you invite hope to spring forth from sorrow when your ego and thoughts would rather strategize against the stillness you need? It is a natural habit to avoid discomfort. It is natural to be lost in your loss, wanting guidance and action. But allowing discomfort to reach into your depths is also as natural as flexing a muscle. Even as a muscle tears, with rest it is repaired, emerging stronger than ever.

Philippians 4:6-7
"Don't worry about anything; instead, pray about everything. Tell God what you need and thank Him for all He has done. Then you will experience God's peace, which exceeds anything we can understand. His peace will guard your hearts and minds as you live in Christ."

For today
It's time to just be. In our rush to recover, we flood our task lists with the hope that each action will restore our hearts or at least keep

us distracted. Instead, let's ask the Holy Spirit to show us the compassion-filled intangibles that keep us grounded. Things we love, require, and long for when the world becomes too much. When everyone needs your attention, what is the non-thing you want the most? Think about concepts, adjectives, and your five senses. You might need quiet; someone else might need loud.

Your new list of what is needed "to-be" comforted and made whole will help you determine which actions belong on the "to-do" list in the wake of your grief, and which do not. Discernment and listening to a still, small voice may seem impossible right now. So instead of avoiding discomfort by numbing, distracting, or acting busy, we can embrace discomfort with patience and focus on the simplest needs. Those who mourn will always be offered comfort from God. Make space for Him to be the comforter.

Day Twenty Five
Move, Change, Grow, and Evolve

"You don't need to see the Invisible String. People who love each
other are always connected by a very special String made of love."
Patricia Karst

In the world of grief management, there has been a strong undercurrent of belief that the traditional process of acceptance requires you to detach from the loss in order to move on. Thankfully, the revolutionary idea of continuing the connection to a loved one after death became popularized in the mid-90s, validating the painful experience of trying to accept or understand a new normal.

Rather than detaching, we can acknowledge that bonds forged in love last forever and find new ways to remain connected and healthy, without believing we are "stuck in our grief forever." A quick side note: "stuck" can only be defined by the griever. If someone else labels you as "stuck," consider inviting them to keep their opinions and assessments to themselves. We move at our own pace.

One of the ways I remain connected to my mom is through cooking. She was an incredible chef, working in the service industry for much of her career. I inherited her 13-inch Zwilling J.A. Henckels chef knife, and when I use or sharpen the blade, I imagine what she would be preparing in her own kitchen based on the weather or the time of year. I laugh every time I crave soup, because it was one of her least favorite things to eat. But making her chicken and dumplings brings me back to my childhood within seconds.

For years, I avoided the knife. I was afraid to drop or damage it or remember too much. Yet now it deepens my connection to her. That knife became a symbol of hope, joy, and a completely natural way to grieve. I cook with my heart and my mom is with me for every cut.

Consider anyone choosing to remarry after the first ended, no matter the reason. Pretending the prior relationship did not exist would be an incredible detriment to the new relationship. If widows are unable to recall their past with joy, or stepchildren cannot express their loneliness, how can they be expected to create healthy attachments to the new people in their lives?

I now use the knife on a daily basis. Each time I sharpen it, I recognize the impermanence of this knife as well. As the shavings fall, I practice gratitude for the time I will have this knife and gentle grace for the time when it will be no more.

What possibility exists if you choose to view your environment in a way that offers new and lasting connection points to the person you lost? We may believe keeping items is the only way to recall the person, and while physical reminders help, they are certainly not the only appropriate method.

Becoming mindful that we are not overly attached to physical items will also serve well as we reframe our present lives. Building a new connection means allowing our memories and thoughts to surface as needed, while still engaging in that which brings us joy and hope. There is no guilt – you are simply recalling the beauty of your connection and allowing the fullness of what was to join you in the present.

Matthew 19:14-15
'But Jesus said, 'Let the children come to me. Don't stop them! For the Kingdom of Heaven belongs to those who are like these children.' And he placed his hands on their heads and blessed them before he left."

For today

I felt great relief when my tears of memories turned from sorrow to gratitude. The avoidance of remembering people I'd lost was the best tool I had to move forward at the time, but avoidance was stealing the very thing I needed to remain connected – my invisible string. This inviting concept from a kid's book reminds me that even as we progress in our growth, we deserve the simplicity of remaining childlike in our faith, hope, and love.

I love the book, "The Invisible String," because when we present heavy topics to children, we do it simply. We invite them to grow from the moral narrative, but we also offer patience and grace-filled comfort while they heal. We must allow the same for ourselves.

How can you extend mercy to yourself today as you heal? Perhaps you can recognize a few items you're holding onto from your loss, and evaluate what they mean. Where do you see your own invisible strings? Set aside a few minutes to exhale and reflect on the beauty and connectedness that remains.

Six
Restorative Grief

Grief trashes our present to the point where we are grasping for our future and excavating our past; as if we can uncover something we missed that will restore the gift of today! Such a belief leaves our present hopeless. This is neither the promise nor the reality, yet this wrong belief can turn our faith into a battlefield instead of a source of restoration. In order to find peace, we need to embrace the promise of hope in our daily lives as a reality, not only as something to come. But how can we embrace our present when we still experience triggers on a daily basis?

There are so many methodologies and theories written to help the bereaved manage their losses. While tips and tools for the moment are crucial, the way forward through ongoing trauma is to have a target in mind. The targets we set are not designed to be goals we reach, but a point in each day for our attention to land when the mind begins firing arrows in all directions. To find restoration through our grief, we must identify our target, acknowledge that it is always moving, and bring grace upon grace into our present moments.

The more time we spend bringing ourselves back to the present moment, the more intentionally we will make decisions about our needs and next steps. Our healing takes the forefront, allowing each wave of unexpected grief to propel us toward shore instead of tossing us about in the surf.

This process is ongoing, never ending, and beautiful if we will allow the honesty of our hearts to receive the gift of comfort. Our lives were designed and created to exist in a flow between heaven and earth – we are created in motion, from the moment the breath of God invades our existence. As we practice stillness of mind, our body remembers its design and healthy movements.

If we can become open to the idea that even through loss we can grow, then we will find ourselves embracing clarity and hope like old friends. Even writing these words takes courage. Grief is not something we enjoy or a topic we want to embrace. And yet, the uncomfortable nature of life is that we are always invited to enter the unknown. How much have we missed by declining this invitation?

Restorative grief allows our hearts to recover and reorganize our lives in a way that accommodates the loss yet still allows peace to reign when it resurfaces. It brings us to the center of the storm, where Comfort Himself awaits us with sight and insight.

The work we do now is building our resilience. By acknowledging our grief, we become aware of the places that need the most humility. We are not releasing our person, our loss, or trying to move on. We are learning to lament and remain present. We are learning to live openhanded with our emotions, our challenges, and our love.

Let's be realistic for a moment. Even with the best intentions in healing, you will probably miss your target. Does that mean you should never take aim? Setting a target (rather than a goal) invites course corrections. Any archer will tell you that while the goal is to hit the center, they must account for many variables as they take aim and still celebrate landing on the target. Even with the most intentional, well-sighted shot, a last-minute external influence can throw the arrow off its path.

Regardless of the variables, the most consistently successful archers never take their eyes from the target. As you are setting your thoughts and intentions toward healing, consider your capacity to remain focused. It may be smaller than you wish, and that is perfectly normal. Your capacity will grow with time—and with every small target that you hit.

We need to learn how to set our aim on our own stories. Denying the pain and confusion of what happens to us steals our ability to comprehend our reality with the understanding of grace. We will never get an answer to the proverbial, "Why?" but we can live within a cultivated peace. We can believe again in the mystery of life and the revelation of who we are becoming. With love at the front, peace to the rear, joy in the moment and patience in each step, we can find restoration.

Day Twenty Six
Overidentifying with Closure

"Closure is a myth, but progress is not."
Frank Ochberg

As we pursue our restoration, we must reject the notion of closure. Closure is a fairytale and right now, our stories are far from whimsical. The idea that like a book, you can finish the grief process and set it upon the shelf feels dismissive of both my story and my emotions. The opposite of closure is openhanded hope.

Often, culture recommends closure because it feels succinct; absolute — final. But what's with the rush? Our overidentification with the need for closure hurries our process, limiting our own ability to hold space and find peace in the present circumstances. Our lives are not a novel to be set aside when the action ends. We are always revising and adding pages.

Rushing into healing for the sake of another seems noble. But is it wise? Is it sustainable? Maybe you're a widowed parent wanting to give their children some idea of normalcy. Maybe you're the child of a bereaved parent, wondering how to get your lives "back on track."

Listen: In grief, your life has jumped the tracks. The path before you? It's forked in more ways than one. But even with an uncharted path ahead, you are not navigating blindly. Closure is a concept built on assumptions that grief is bad and must come to an end. But when we look ahead, we are reconstructing a future and a story with a baseline of hope. Grief is not a moral failure; it's a fact of life.

Maybe you feel differently; perhaps you do feel closure in some way about your grief, and that is fine. Our processes are as unique as our DNA. But if we are looking to navigate our grief differently and outside of the popular assumptions of our culture, then we must risk exploring that closure is a construct we have allowed that no longer serves. Maybe it never did.

Has the pursuit of closure complicated your healing? How has a lack of closure changed the way you feel about yourself? We may find that we deny our emotions are valid, or even our behaviors as natural when we are too busy writing our closing statements.

Nancy Berns, author of 'Closure: The Rush to End Grief and What It Costs Us' writes, "People don't need closure. That's just one way to talk about grief. You don't need it to begin healing and to find progress in learning how to live with a loss." We have spent all this time reframing our grief within the true narrative that God loves us, did not take our person from us, and is mourning with us. In the same moments, He is bringing us a new hope.

Romans 15:13
"I pray that God, the source of hope, will fill you completely with joy and peace because you trust in Him. Then you will overflow with confident hope through the power of the Holy Spirit."

For today

The actions we take in search of closure can be redirected to instead envision a future of hope. We want to restore our hearts toward ourselves in the present, coming to like ourselves even in our sadness. From that position of vulnerable self-acceptance, we do not aim to bring our grief to an end. We aim to be at peace, restored to wholeness in the present time. We have not failed if we mourn our loss decades later; we've simply healed to a point and now have the chance to heal further.

Anxiety and grief are stifling. If we need fresh air, we go outside or open a window. We literally reject closure. Today, open a window or a door. Stand at the threshold and exhale, imagining the path before you as open, hopeful, inviting, and ready when you are.

Day Twenty Seven
Permission to Circle Back

"Resolution? I hate the word. I use the term 'accommodate,' because at different points in time you can have accommodated the loss, made room for it in your life, and have come to a relative peace with it, but then something else can bring it up again later on. Grief is something that continues to get reworked."
Therese Rando

Part of the intention with this work is to create a resource for every "stage" of your grief. Whether it has been a day or years, the spiraling nature of grief means we are always looking at our lives with this filter of loss. But it does not mean the filter must remain heavy and grainy, distorting the way we see life day to day.

One of my minors in college was photography, and I shot with a vintage Canon AE-1 SLR from the 1970s. I loved the manual manipulations I could create both while shooting and printing in the darkroom, but especially when I used light and filters to create more than a straightforward capture.

The filters we apply to our vision can be the emphasis or blockage to our sight as we observe and process the world we now inhabit. In grief, our tendency to look back in sorrow or forward in anxiety is why we need to cultivate a method of remaining present, as often as we can.

But to dismiss our hindsight or prior methods as outdated means we are discarding them because they must lack value. But the tools we've used served a purpose. As we transcend and heal, we must gently observe where we were in our grief process and include that which served well, releasing the rest without judgment.

We do not arrive at wholeness. We work toward it, as often as we can. But when the relative peace we've found starts to waver, we deserve to approach our lives with the same openhearted hospitality we would offer an old friend. Creating space for ourselves to revisit our anger, depression, or confusion is natural and necessary. It's the same reason we reread our favorite books; they introduced something new that carried great value. The way we experience and embrace our losses can do the same.

This is not to say that our loss is valuable, and yet even in absence, there is matter. On my left arm, I have a tattoo of a bird carved out of negative space within a flame. The substance discovered in subtraction is complex, nuanced, and wildly intentional. Learning to observe the negative space with curiosity, even as it flares unexpectedly, will highlight different moments for healing that you previously overlooked. Appreciating the beauty of negative space does not replace what you lost, but it can be significant in your revelation and healing.

Proverbs 3:5-6
"Trust in the Lord with all your heart; do not depend on your own understanding. Seek his will in all you do, and he will show you which path to take."

For today

Circle back! Take time today to reread a journal entry from earlier in your grief story. Approach your own words as if they are a letter from your best friend. Put compassion at the front and shove judgment out the door!

Ask God to illuminate your words and trust Him to give you sight and insight. What did you previously believe about your grief and your loss that you've come to understand differently? Is there an area of your loss that confused you that now carries clarity? How can you find intentionality in the negative space in your life, right now, even as you grieve your loss? What new understanding can you gain that you missed the first time around? Allow grace and wisdom to change your mind, if needed, for peace. You can trust God to keep you as you circle around for new and deeper healing. You can trust yourself to expand and include what matters.

Day Twenty Eight
Engaging Flow

"The only way to make sense out of change is to plunge into it, move
with it, and join the dance."
Alan Wilson Watts

I crave the experience of déjà vu. When your mind suddenly
transports you with this inner knowing and deep familiarity, it can be
both unsettling and comforting. Personally, I consider the sense of
remembrance as a confirmation that I am in the flow of my life,
precisely where I am called to exist. That moment is a promise made
manifest; even when it hurts.

I also love when I am meditating on a certain scripture or concept
and find it continues to arise in conversation, readings, or podcasts.
When the noises around me create symphonic harmonies with my
own thoughts, the delight of being in unity overtakes the fear of an
echo chamber. As I purposefully surround my life with creative
people who embody a different perspective than my own, I am
challenged and astounded when we find not only common
understanding, but unified thoughts.

This is how God engages our mind with His promises in the world.
He is uniquely manifesting His presence everywhere around us, and
yet in our distraction, confusion, and biases, we miss a lot (to say the
least). However, as all of us grievers know, the Great Slow Down of
time in grief invites us into that Matrix-like film style of observation
at a slower pace. We notice things we missed. As our conscious

minds start to understand the connectedness of creation, we realize we are in the flow of the spirit.

The Holy Spirit is unhindered by our emotions, barriers, or biases. Becoming sensitive to the way She shifts our comprehension is crucial to healing. In grief, I believe we are uniquely invited to engage the Holy Spirit in a way we cannot prior to experiencing loss. As the comforter, She remains closer than ever with gentle wisdom. Grieving hearts are searching for meaning, and in the movement of Her embrace, she reveals deeper aspects of God's character.

It is crucial to engage the flow of our lives. As we are reorganizing the details, God wants to move with us, unveiling His face again and again to demonstrate the wild generosity and unrestrained grace. Holding the details of our stories lightly means living openhanded, with clear eyes and a trusting heart. Our empty handedness in loss transforms into a sign of hope that we will receive something good; that we will find meaning in our lives, despite having suffered such great loss.

Engaging flow allows for gentle movement through our loss. We notice the waves approaching, welcoming them as an old friend with familiarity. We are equipped to wade through lament, stronger than before because we have embraced the plunge into the unknown and know we will breathe again.

Micah 6:8
"He has told you what is good, and what has he asked of you? To do justice, to love mercy, and to walk humbly with your God."

For today

I want to invite you to listen to music by the artist Kinnship. This artist created an electronic, meditative style of music that allows one's thoughts to simply float. You can find his work on Apple Music, Spotify, YouTube, etc. and I highly recommend the songs, "Dipped My Toes," or my personal favorite, "Homingbird."

Allowing our barricades to fall means we do not continue to avoid or press against but lean into the presence of God as we heal.

I want us to experience what it feels like to flow through movement with no true directives. Feel free to experience other music as well but try to select instrumental or pieces with only a few words. Invite the Holy Spirit to bring sight of where you have prevented flow from moving freely. In this moment of release, I believe you will experience a new level of connectivity in body, mind, and spirit to the justice, mercy, and humility of heaven.

Embrace the drift. Expand your lungs. Move your body. Wiggle your toes. Close your eyes. Find your smile.

Day Twenty Nine
Rest, Work, Beloved

"Grief by itself is not a lesson, but there are lessons to be learned in grief."
Megan Devine

Sometimes the work of a grief coach and the griever can trip over this concept of "doing the work." We want to take responsibility for our lives, and in doing so, can steamroll over the very rest we need. But there is a third way of existence that encompasses rest and work as partners. When we begin to believe that our natural state of being is beloved, our focus changes. Rather than trying to cultivate rest or constantly produce, we can explore the motives for our action with empathy for ourselves.

Doing the work of grief means leaning into the difficult, complex, and uncomfortable emotions. When we run full steam into "the work," we risk crashing into a brick wall. Pain explodes when there is no rest. On the contrary, when we spend so much time trying to cultivate rest, it can feel like we never "do enough of the work." This is where "shoulding" and shame creep back into the narrative.

But if we accept the lesson that we are beloved, we are catapulted into a new plane of existence. Our story changes. If I am beloved, then I find rest in knowing that I have access to the mental inner peace needed to "do the work." When it becomes too much, I can step back without anxiety that the work is undone. I've done enough, right where I am, with what I have. I am still beloved, whether I feel a release or feel stuck.

The greatest lesson we can learn in grief is not that we needed to lose something to gain. In grief, we tend to minimize our pain and our value to show others we're healing. What are we trying to prove? We are worth the time it takes to heal, no matter how long that is. We are worth the investment of love; the slow movement through relationships that makes us feel heard, seen, and known. Uncovering our own value and believing we are worthy of love is the biggest lesson I believe that we can take from grief. When we risk love, we risk grief, too. Grief is a demonstration that we loved each other deeply. We were willing to be vulnerable and show up to live life fully.

When we get wild in that love, our emotions get wild with us. Something about grief tricks us into accepting a dampening of our wild. That our emotions need to stay small and controlled — as if there were an appropriate response to grief.

Accepting our wild heart allows us to find the restrictions we've placed on our grief and begin to express ourselves more honestly. Our love deserves to express itself, whether that is through the blowouts in anger or tears of laughter. Let us invite our thawing hearts to accept the warmth of an embrace that says, "You are beloved."

2 Corinthians 4:8-9
"We are pressed on every side by troubles, but we are not

crushed. We are perplexed, but not driven to despair. We are hunted down, but never abandoned by God."

For today

When we know we are beloved, we will trust another to join us in our process. We need others to show up and as adults, we have the benefit of knowing we can ask for help. Today, ask for help. When your big emotions are like a tsunami, being met by a friend with still waters creates an opportunity for a shared experience.

In a relationship, we continually influence one another; here, we can allow ourselves to be influenced by one demonstrating the very peace we desire. Allow a person you trust to show up for you, offering their strength and connection through listening, empathy, nearness, and curiosity. Where you are struggling to believe the best about yourself, and your validity in this process, you can borrow the confidence and belief of your friend on your behalf. Let them love you well; let them see your wild. You are beloved.

Day Thirty
The Clarity Winter Brings

"Out of the smoking ruins came cries of lamentation and confession,
and the daring hope of restoration."
Graeme Goldsworthy

The stillness of winter may seem cold, confusing, and lonely. But as
we gaze through the bare trees and barren landscapes, perhaps we
will notice how much further we can see. For years now, I have
written poetically through my grief. Themes of winter seem to wind
through each one, simply because I see winter as a tucking away,
restorative buckling down of the world. It is the introspective,
necessary time to reflect and allow my roots to go deeper.

"But I want to breathe that ancient air, ripe with possibilities of an
unfolding world. When you declared darkness to take the back seat
and summoned oceans from dry beds, You were creating a world
You knew would fall away, hell-bent on destroying itself before it
discovered the way home. You've been running toward me,
disheveled and disgraced, longer than I've been alive. You run with
abandon for every heart that just wants to stop hurting."

This is the time we get to practice our faith – believing that even in
the emptiest of worlds, there is a promise in pursuit of our hearts,
carrying restoration. It is in the presence of grief that so many well-
meaning people (and too often, Christians) cause near irreparable
damage to our souls and our faith when offering platitudes and ill-
conceived measures of comfort. And yet, because we do not want to

be alone, we accept the broken comfort anyway, praying it will help more than harm.

I think we accept the counterfeit comfort because we do not want to sit alone. But if we cannot practice our peace today with ourselves, we will miss out on what the Holy Spirit is trying to restore to us in this moment. Too much focus on the memories of yesterday or the unknown of tomorrow steals our ability to say yes to what we need today.

Finding restoration through grief is the ultimate gift to our souls. The work it takes to remain still with ourselves through the pain and discomfort is the clarity and healing we need to find restoration. Our bodies, minds, and hearts are revealed to us as a new thing; wholly different than before because the absence in our story is real. And yet, even as we know there is no substitute for the loss we've suffered, we have learned to inhale the promise of peace. It is in this place of peace where we can learn to say what we need, what we want, and what we require. We speak with confidence and clarity because we have found our voice and regained our breath.

John 20:22

"Then he breathed on them and said, 'Receive the Holy Spirit.'"

For today

The sacred Tetragrammaton is one of my favorite and most intimate meditations. The name of God in Hebrew is spelled YHWH (yod, he, vay, and he), and most pronounce it "Yahweh." Historically, it is believed that God's name cannot be written or spoken, and these three letters are the only consonants in the Hebrew alphabet that are breathed – the lips and tongue take no part.

We start this life with breath filling our lungs like a gasp; life ends when it leaves us. God's first and most important gift to us is the impartation of His breath into our bodies. It was so important to Him that we literally have the chance to say His name with every breath we take. Don't let grief steal yours for another moment. Life came from God, and His breath within us sustains us through all. There is incredible healing in the breath. Today, your challenge is to remain with your breath and meditate on the name of God.

Alongside this breathing exercise, identify what you need (if you have not yet already done so). What do you need? What do you want? What do you require? Spell it out with clarity and confidence that you have the right and the resilience to ask and receive.

Day Thirty One
Understanding Loss in Context of Hope

"Death leaves a heartache no one can heal; love leaves a memory
no one can steal."
Richard Puz

Our move through acceptance into a position of growth no longer carries judgment, but curiosity and compassion. Throughout this work, we have practiced tools to create self-compassion and hold space for ourselves, which is the first necessary step to becoming a safe space in grief for others. At times, the idea of sitting still and allowing grief, tears, or anger to surface created great discomfort. But these hard acts of discomfort are the teeth-gritting breakthroughs we need to embrace if we want to heal from our grief in a way that helps us evolve through the pain. Here, we will continue to expand and include.

Our intention in embracing our losses is not to move on, but forward. We are becoming flexible, growing and expanding our boundaries. We are growing to accept the new thing we cannot control, but embrace. While we most often do not want the grief that accompanies change, this is our chance to understand the grief better. There is no change in life that does not have some layer of grief attached.

In the book of John, Jesus discusses the impending death of Lazarus, explaining the death of His friend will be to the purpose of God's glory. This scripture has been taken from context often enough to make a point that God orchestrates our losses intentionally. This is rejection and failure to heal in grief; the wrong belief that God is lazy and detached, unloving and unkind enough to take someone we dearly love. How can we accept our losses with God as the comforter if it seems even God is heartless or indifferent?

Digging into the truth of scripture relies on the context of it — allowing the stories to remain in context is the same practice of integrity we must focus on as we begin to unpack and understand our own stories. Without a proper setting, the plot floats freely. Imagine trying to understand the tales of Middle Earth if Tolkien hadn't described the political unrest in the land; or the nuance of Narnia without the visceral details of The Dawn Treader.

If we believe that Jesus embodies the promise of resurrection, then the context of Lazarus' passing served the purpose because Jesus was already intent on resurrecting His friend as demonstration of His total authority over death. The way we can evolve through the pain of our grief is by understanding the immensity of our loss and allowing it to remain in context. This protects our memory and the lasting love we will feel for those who've gone from our lives. Catastrophizing, blaming, ignoring, and hiding are all habits of those who are not able to internalize the lesson of John 11 — God is always listening to the heart cries of His people and in response, He releases new life. Sometimes in resurrection, but always in restoration.

John 11:44
"Jesus said to them, 'Take off the grave clothes and let him go.'"

For today

Making space for God as the comforter means we must choose to believe that He is as loving as He claims. This alone can be the lynchpin for someone's faith falling apart in grief. Do we have the capacity to trust God? Explore your foundation. Healing in your grief may require you to question some of the hard and fast rules you've carried your whole life. Perhaps that's why the losses aren't making any sense. Choosing to believe differently than we were raised or than we have physical evidence for is a sign that our beliefs are moving toward the more solid ground of faith. We don't need all the answers to find peace or clarity. We need confidence that we can trust a Creator that we cannot control.

As we curiously lean toward our own growth through our loss, let's ask questions of ourselves that challenge our beliefs about God's character in the context of grief. Read John 11. Without censoring or editing, observe your response to the story. Is your response what you expected? Why or why not? Give yourself the grace to accept there is no right way to respond to this chapter; only the way that moves you forward in accepting hope as offered.

Seven
Platitudes *and* Toxic Positivity

The remaining chapters of this book will hopefully break apart a few of the concepts discussed throughout the 31 days, including platitudes, minimizing, boundary setting, and more. A lot of the ideas are familiar but misunderstood. With a little grace for ourselves, we can become the helpers we always imagined we were. We can learn to navigate the discomfort of grieving aloud in a world that would rather we remain quiet in our pain.

Platitudes

Platitudes are the most familiar way we offer comfort to those in mourning. We introduce these ingrained, pithy phrases without thinking. Let's unpack the complications caused by platitudes and hopefully, gain a little mindfulness the next time we open our hearts to offer a word of advice.

Most of the time, grievers can trust that those sharing platitudes do not mean any additional harm – quite the opposite. Still, they consistently cause more damage than we realize. Why do we feel so driven to offer platitudes to someone we love? Why do we believe that when someone shows their most vulnerable side, we have to say something to decrease the discomfort?

We are a culture obsessed with self-preservation. We defend our ideas passionately and often speak without thinking. Why? Because we hate discomfort. We have no idea how to sit in silence. We do not know how to compassionately hold space without trying to exert control over our appearance or what another believes about us. This translates so easily to grievers and grief-supporters. When the circumstance becomes tense, we will often say whatever we can to get out of it as quickly as possible. Avoidance feels safer than discomfort.

Have you ever withheld your own story of grief because the response received would cause a deeper wound? Maybe you're offered an anecdote from the listener's life. Maybe they say, "I totally understand. I know exactly how that feels." In the noble attempt to help a person feel heard, we inadvertently minimize their story by hijacking the attention to our own experience. We attempt to silence the pain of another to preserve our sense of comfort. It is never an intentional act — and that's the point.

We must become intentional in the way we serve and hope to encourage grievers. It is so easy to be swept away in the same method of "helping" that seems to have always worked. We share to relate and demonstrate understanding, but the truth is, we will never understand. Even if we believe we've experienced the same type of loss, we don't know what another person is going through unless we ask questions. Even then, our empathy is too easily shoved aside by a misguided belief that we must provide comfort.

But what if we just stopped talking? What would happen if we just sat down next to them and stayed quiet? Could things possibly get worse?

Consider a time you were grieving and decided to speak vulnerably. Did you expect the listener to make you feel better or fix what was broken? More likely, you wanted to be seen – to be heard. When we are hurting, we want to give context for our pain. Often the very telling of our story provides context for ourselves that we missed. Grief breaks our connections to the world around us. Telling our story to the uncomfortable among us can explain why we do not laugh as often or have as much energy. Our hearts feel broken. When a griever becomes vulnerable and provides context, it removes pretense and expectation; in this place, we can live and grieve without shame. The context for our story breaks assumptions and creates real understanding.

Inviting Simplicity

It is difficult to remember what we should or should not say. If nothing else, it's okay to say something awkward like, "I have no idea how to respond." Being awkward is natural, inviting, and endearing. The person you are hoping to comfort will appreciate that you chose to feel uncomfortable instead of offering a platitude.

Almost everything about grief is awkward. But we spend so much time searching for comfort that we can forget about the power found in discomfort as well. Cleaning out a loved one's home is awkward – bedside tables, anyone? Finding someone's diary is awkward. Picking out an urn is awkward.

Acknowledging and making space for the discomfort in grief is crucial. If this is the first time you've supported someone with a loss, it will be awkward. You may be surprised by how little or how much they need you. Or maybe you've done this before yet showed up with your own motives and intentions (this is known as centering our own needs in another's narrative). Maybe you caused more damage in your wake.

Discomfort is the seat of deep revelation. In the season when we feel powerless, it is often because we have been addicted to the seeming certainty of life. Our self-preservation has kept us tucked away, secure in a bubble of belief that we are always safe. But when that safety, certainty, or security is threatened (especially through loss of life), the idea of impermanence is the easiest to reject. No one wants to feel uncertain, but by allowing discomfort we can find our true footing. This isn't the gospel of silver linings; far from it. This is a reminder that many of our best stories have grown from a willingness to be uncomfortable, even for a moment.

I'll never forget when I was a few hours into labor with our daughter. My mom was standing at my side, holding my hand. She squeezed tightly and said, "You're almost done honey! The pain is almost over." My doctor calmly explained that she was wrong, and it would not feel better soon. In fact, I could expect worse pain to come. At the time, I couldn't help but laugh. I knew the heart behind my mom's words. I saw her discomfort with not being able to prevent my pain. I deeply appreciated her intention to bring me comfort. But being a straightforward person, I also appreciated the truth from my doctor. This is going to hurt, but oh baby, it will be so worth the pain at the end.

If we have the capacity to see grief in this framework, we can choose to endure the heaviness without dismissing hope. We can be awkward and uncomfortable together.

This is redemption time. The following list of platitudes is not complete. Some are related to faith; some are arbitrary comments looking to lay blame where it does not belong. But with each, try on the alternatives offered. The "I love you and don't know what to say, but I'm here," is a solid standby.

When your intentions are pure, most grieving people will forgive you, even when you make a mistake. But let's love the grievers (and ourselves) well enough to learn better first. Let's give them an opportunity to enjoy our company instead of figuring out how to forgive our missteps. Instead of "encouragement," let's try affirmations of love. This takes practice, and at first, you will get it wrong. But the grace to course correct means that if you notice yourself offering a platitude, be courageous and loving enough to apologize. Stop mid-sentence if you must, explaining that you noticed a platitude emerging from your mouth, and try again. I guarantee your griever will appreciate your honesty, integrity, and willingness to be a listener instead of one trying to repair what feels broken.

Instead of... They're in a better place now.
Try... Your life together was beautiful and I'm with you.

Instead of... Everything happens for a reason.
Try... Losing them is terrible and I'm so sorry.

Instead of... At least they are no longer hurting.
Try... The pain you feel is real, I see you, and I'm here.

Instead of... Time heals all wounds.
Try... I'm with you for as long as it takes.

Instead of... God needed an angel/has an angel.
Try... Will you tell me a story about something they loved?

Instead of... I cannot imagine how difficult this is.
Try... I am here to listen if you want to talk about it.

Instead of... They would want you to be happy.
Try... How do you want to feel today and what can we do about it together? I'm here for all of it, if you'll have me.

Centering

Centering is how we adjust to the discomfort and realign with our personal idea of feeling good. When someone else is vulnerable with us about their pain, we are being invited into a sacred moment. Centering occurs when we rush into the sacred moment without being mindful. We try to relate or show support without asking questions. Our curiosity is set aside, and we may even try to use the moment to our advantage by showing off what great support we can provide.

As grievers, we are trying to believe the best about people who want to offer support, but it's hard — especially when the offers of comfort are inappropriate or harmful. It can be complicated to know if you've offended a griever because often, we won't say anything about those harmful statements. We don't want to "rock the boat" relationally because we hardly have the emotional space for simple conversations. Instead, we stay quiet and gently pull away. By offering advice or resources without asking first, you place yourself in the center of the circumstance. It implies that you are uncomfortable being unable to fix the problem and struggle with allowing another to continue feeling heavy or unsettled.

I don't want to dismiss your heart to support or discourage you from showing up for someone in need. My hope is to bring greater awareness to those in positions of support that we must truly serve the needs of others and not our own ego.

We need to become curious about our intention in offering help. As we do so, we will become better helpers by truly investigating our motives and intention through the lens of centering. Recently, I chose to share a vulnerable story of my loss. While a few people were able to acknowledge and offer kindness, one used it as an opportunity. Rather than ask what I might need in the moment, the person assumed and offered a resource. Centering leads us as helpers to believe we have an answer for a question that was not asked.

As soon as this person offered the resource, the empathy offered became sympathy. The extended prayers felt empty because I felt a need to defend my emotional state as valid. Grievers need to know it is okay that they're not okay. In the rush to offer support, we can dismiss without the intention of doing so. Simply having a solution does not mean your solution is needed or appropriate.

How can we show up and offer empathy without centering our perspectives, ideas, or stories? By showing up where they are starting with a heart to learn, not teach or correct. To risk being misunderstood or corrected.

Ask what may seem obvious: Is this person asking a question to gain support? It can be easy to read between the lines and determine if a griever may need something, but unless they are being explicit in their request, we can assume the griever is being honest instead. Grievers need to practice being direct with their requests to avoid resentment. We supporters need to practice becoming curious without judgment. If our questions are loaded with assumptions, ready to correct or condemn, we will likely lose access to this person and deepen their wounds. Our role is to believe the storyteller — to accept their conclusions with heart-forward responses and to drop our desire to be right, to guide, or to teach.

Obtain Permission

Attempting to decenter our support can seem dismissive of our nature. Maybe we are supporters who have great discernment or insight into the circumstances. This isn't to dismiss intuition as harmful, but to cultivate conversation around intuition as a standard practice. It is perfectly acceptable to offer your support or resources by asking permission to do so. It will sound something like, "I would love to tell you about a book I read that helped me through grief, when you're ready or interested." It's not about sales; you do not need to convince someone to let you support their healing. Unless you do, in which case... this conversation about centering is one you may need to reread.

It is also important to invite feedback! Ask whether they found your support to be meaningful or helpful. Let the griever know you want to come alongside them in a way they appreciate, rather than what is convenient for you. Remember, grievers do not want to rock the boat. We want to find still waters. Inviting our feedback means you care about how we're feeling throughout the process; not just when grief is new or the position of "Chief Grief Supporter" appears vacant.

Offering Vulnerability

I owe it to myself and other people to be honest. What I do not owe is my vulnerability. My vulnerability is a gift and a source of strength. We think we must live as "open books," but this is just a grasp at security. What we call an "open book" is often a safe presentation of our story – the carefully curated pages to expose and share with the people we deem are safe enough or from whom we want approval.

If you are in the position to receive someone's vulnerability, be gentle. It's easy to reply quickly with comforting thoughts, but this is how platitudes ruin the ever-deepening relationship between grievers and supporters.

Grief is rife with insecurity; to believe that a griever owes their vulnerability is taking advantage of the hurting. But allowing a griever to be honest, no matter how uncomfortable you may feel, is one of the greatest gifts you can offer. In the same way, your returned vulnerability (relinquishing control over the comfort level of the moment) is more appreciated than you can know.

In loss, the truth of our impermanence and lack of control over the world sends us spiraling. Looking for comfort in the people around us makes sense. But if I trust you enough to share that I've lost someone dear, then the greatest gift you can give me is your silence. Picture the space bar on a keyboard. Without it, our words would jumble into a mess of nonsense. We do not live our lives as a run-on sentence; we live with space to breathe and exhale. Both are necessary. Silence and/or active listening are gifts in themselves (more on active listening soon).

My role as a grief coach is to act in accordance with my values when I hear a vulnerable and honest story from another human. I hold space by allowing silence to linger. When we speak too quickly, our gut instinct is to pray or declare comfort. But this is because we have forgotten that love is always willing to sit in the mud. **We have forgotten the value of lament.**

In our hurry to heal, we misunderstand the purpose of a scab on a wound. Healing takes more than time. Even as it heals, the wound might itch. We could scratch and disrupt the process, leaving scars. Healing takes intention and a willingness to let discomfort do the work on our behalf.

Curiosity Without Judgment

One of my favorite lessons in grieving with others comes from receiving non-judgmental curiosity. A dear friend would check in occasionally and she always had a question ready. "Tell me about your mom. What is one thing you miss about her today?"

I had no obligation to respond, but the invitation helped me feel seen, known, and loved. In our attempt to show up for others, we may offer platitudes but miss the simplicity of offering our curiosity and time instead.

In the beginning, recounting stories about my loss was too painful. But the way my friend asked questions, patiently awaiting my answer, lessened my fear of receiving platitudes in response. The best part of her questions was her offering at the end of each story.

"Thank you for sharing with me. I love you."

When another person can be curious and compassionate for our healing, we can learn to offer ourselves the same. Before rushing to the next section, take a few minutes to ruminate. This work requires your full attention and intention to have any lasting impact. Embracing the awkward, honest, and vulnerable moments in grief invites healing. It invites intimacy. It creates depth in our souls that other relationships will mimic in response. Humility is the way forward.

Faith and Spiritual Bypassing as Platitudes

Any time religion is used to justify or explain loss, someone is going to come unhinged. If you have a deep relationship with the person grieving, you may feel comfortable using scripture as an affirmation that they are not alone. But repeating the Sermon on the Mount in the moment of sorrow will do little good (and often, harm).

There is nothing that feels blessed when we are in mourning. In the middle of our sorrow, a reminder that God is blessing us can make those blessings feel like a curse. Allowing us to feel deeply and work through anger is crucial to healing (and to finding any gratitude for blessings in our future).

Using scriptures to quiet the crying minimizes our grief. This is also known as "spiritual bypassing." In asking us to remember the promises of scripture, you are communicating that our grief is a distraction from our faith. This is not true. We cannot deny our humanity or our real emotions simply because they cause discomfort. Offering an opinion that God will use this loss to catalyze our growth causes more people to walk away from faith than anything else I've encountered in my grief work thus far. Often, grievers do not realize they are carrying the wounds of spiritual bypassing but may subconsciously hold this behavior as valuable. Have you ever believed something like, "If I can pray enough, this pain will leave?"

And herein lies the problems with the idea of silver linings. They're platitudes in disguise! In the same way I can relate to and apply a platitude to my own understanding, I may eventually find silver linings in my process. But if someone else suggests that I should be looking for the good in my loss, there is a real chance I will miss something I need to heal. We can't look for silver linings in someone else's timeframe. Healing in grief is the same – the timeline of the griever is paramount – no matter what religious beliefs you want to apply to the loss.

When we are in community, spiritual bypassing can look like support. This is where we must apply our discernment and engage our own hearts in the grieving process. There will be individuals still trying to affirm their own understanding of loss and grief. Those are not people who can hold space for us long term, and that's okay. But without self-awareness, we may lend our story to their process without honoring what we actually need.

It is not likely that other people are trying to intentionally control what you believe about loss. But spiritual bypassing can make us feel like others are questioning our process, our perspectives, or even our emotions. In the vulnerable place of grief, spiritual bypassing becomes even more difficult to identify.

I understand we want to lead hope-filled, inspiring lives. But ultimately, it is crucial that we do the work to reframe our grief to serve our own healing first. The desire to hold space for others is noble, good, and true work. But without first inhaling, we could never offer breath to another. Learning to notice, disable, and unpack spiritual bypassing is powerful work that allows you to create and hold healthy boundaries. Identifying spiritual bypassing is crucial to our healing, regardless of what faith we carry or whether we desire to remain in a faith community. Unchecked, spiritual bypassing can lead our grief process down a path of toxicity, formed in our beliefs and manifested in how we treat ourselves and others through healing. It leads us to believe damaging, destructive platitudes as gospel truths, dismissing our humanity as a distraction and our grief as unworthy of attention.

For far too long, I believed my lack of faith was at the root of my mom's illness and untimely death. I can name no individual who said such a thing directly, but there was a part of me that believed it was true because of how poorly the structure of my faith has been able to address grief beyond platitudes and prayer.

As with all belief systems, we are evolving humans searching for meaning in the world. Loss can upend our understanding of life. As we move toward healing, we must remember how to hold our heart, mind, body, and spirit in high regard. We are a part of creation; a greater narrative than our own. Regardless of what faith we proclaim (or none at all), we must do a better job loving ourselves and others through the depth of loss.

Reconciling Causation vs. Correlation

Spiritual bypassing and platitudes are most often damaging because they confuse causation with correlation. The grief world is full of direction on how to support the grieving without exacerbating their pain, but no advice is universal. For example, many of the platitudes listed before were recently spoken to me as an honest expression of one woman's grief story. She carries each statement in her bones, and without hesitation would offer each as an encouragement to the next person in pain. She truly believed what she was saying, which is meaningful! Where her statements become platitudes of pain is in the intention. She shared with deep affirmation of her process and story. But for most, we have to dig a little deeper and know what we're saying and why.

Knowing the difference between correlation and causation as we speak can be the balm that soothes instead of making our griever feel the burn. Reading the platitudes previously listed triggered a feeling or a reaction. **How can we find the meaning on either side of our emotional reaction?** By exploring the differences between causation and correlation. Distinguishing the two will help us understand why a platitude might encourage some and damage others. Then we can make better decisions about how we speak about grief. While it is not our role to correct another's thought process each time they share, learning the difference between causation and correlation as it pertains to grief can help us offer loving support without causing additional damage.

Platitudes can imply that death/loss is a necessary offering to the universe/God/divine plan to move our self-centered story forward. Karma demands recompense. The volcano demands a sacrifice. God needs our obedience. The person who died or the relationship lost was a distraction or roadblock to our growth.

As the griever, we want to know that our loss was not in vain. There must be a rationale behind our grief that we can take as proof that we will be okay. These statements can dismiss the value of the other party. They also remove our responsibility to self-actualization. It's easier to blame someone else for our lack of vision or passion in life. Have you ever heard a spouse say, "We're just focusing on their career right now?" It's the same idea. Being supportive in a healthy relationship does not mean minimizing your existence to offer support. This is also how spiritual bypassing creates deeper wounds in grief. To call upon the silver linings of the loss rationalizes the pain as necessary for a "blessed future," which is never going to be the case.

The reason for the death/loss is that life is ephemeral. Regardless of your belief system, all things in life are impermanent (even inside reincarnation). Learning to reckon with the uncertainty of our next breath allows us to live breathing deeply, despite great loss. If we can comprehend our own fleeting existence, we can look at each relationship with discernment and appreciation. In fact, the research completed by Elisabeth Kubler-Ross that resulted in her framework of five grief stages was done in the context of her work with terminally-ill patients. While the process applies so poorly to the living, those wrestling with the concept of their own impermanence found comprehension and some clarity. Loss becomes a necessary experience to examine. Grief happens to us all.

We would never admit this, but we love using another person as our excuse to hold back on our dreams. One person's death is not the reason we have freedom. When we tie our storyline to another, we create dependence. While it is true that great loss is often a catalyst toward the new (I'm living proof), I could just as easily have chosen to pursue grief work without losing my mom. Her loss is not the reason I'm here. It is the reason I remain when it becomes overwhelming. I see greater value in this work now, but not because I lost a parent. Causation requires a direct association to the outcome that could not have otherwise occurred. Consider the fact that in summer months, studies have documented an increase in crime rates as well as ice cream consumption. Does one cause the other? Highly unlikely. But without the context of these studies, events, and consideration of the context for each result, we cannot offer a positive conclusion.

And this is true of grief. There are so many variables involved that to reduce our comfort to a simple formula or platitude is to deny the complexity of our stories. But if we understand that no answer will satisfy us, we can become the few who offer support that is needed, valued, and desired in the aftermath of great loss.

Warning: It can be tempting to correct someone in grief when they offer a platitude of their own to express how *they* are coping with their loss. Don't do it. Unless you've been explicitly requested to be a person who speaks influentially into their life (and you would know), then assume you do not have the right to cross that boundary. Trying to correct someone who believes differently than you about grief is a surefire way to be banished to the outer circles of their life, let alone their grief.

The other day, a woman interacted with me online, assuming my openness in storytelling was an invitation to direct, guide, and interrogate my thought process. **It was not.** My hackles raised and immediately I became defensive. This feeling is common: We don't like being told what to do. And yet, we do invite a few trusted people into the vulnerable places in our lives, like a best friend or coach. But just because I'm a coach does not mean I'm your coach. I won't fill that role unless we have an agreement. The same is true of relationships. Grief is a time in life when those boundaries are either highlighted as strong or shattered by mistrust or abuse of your access.

Platitudes usually come out in the form of trying to fill a role that we have not been invited to fill. So, as you gain awareness of your own understanding in grief and how platitudes work, be mindful of your relationship to the people you want to comfort. It can make all the difference.

One last method of offering platitudes that we should discuss is commonly known as "toxic positivity." Despite how often we may hear this phrase, we likely need clarity around the concept. The goal of this positivity mindset is moving on. It ensures that only good vibes are invited forward, never allowing or making space for perspectives that do not inherently promote positivity and hopeful mantras. When I was in college, I earned a C- on a paper in a geology course. I hated that course, and studied as hard as I could with all my other work. Still, I'll never forget how an acquaintance reacted to my news: "Oh my gosh! A C- isn't a big deal! You still passed!"

I remember her shrill voice like it was yesterday. We weren't friends and I wasn't talking to her when she responded. She just happened to be standing nearby. And for some reason, she felt it was her role to show up for me. Where I needed to be heard, she needed to be positive.

Toxic positivity is robbing our hearts of the ability to feel our feelings. There is a time and place for hopeful encouragement, but when a heart lays raw before you with vulnerability, jabbing a foam finger and yelling, "Go team!" will get you ejected from the game before halftime.

When we witness pain or disappointment, it is not our job to offer comfort. It is our role and highest calling to learn how to sit with ourselves first. To know our feelings by name and to give them a chance to exist. Even as the woman in my story meant well by her kind words, she also steamrolled her own discomfort. Forget that she wasn't invited to the conversation. Her interjection stopped all other responses. As if nothing else needed to be said; this woman failed to actively listen, and encouraged the sad person by reframing without permission. Her goal seemed to be for our little group to move onto the next thing.

Moving on is the goal of toxic positivity. Grievers can recognize the platitudes like a tiger's stripes and yet, we still struggle to let the well-intentioned "encouragement" pass without adding to our pain. We have practiced listening to ourselves, our emotions, and our needs. We have learned how to frame our stories in the context of yet, and know that in our own timing, we are learning how to tread water.

Knowing how to correct the overgeneralized happy vibes allows us freedom to be human. That does not mean we must feel sad all the time; it means we must have the chance to feel sad.

Active Listening

Any time you are choosing to show up for someone, no matter their situation, your role is as an observer. If your goal is to encourage others, then you must plan to listen more than you speak.

My favorite way to describe this is from the Pixar movie, "Inside Out." I think about it daily! I told you earlier; I've cried with every viewing. The writers handle loss, grief, trauma, growth, and maturity with an incredibly gentle hand!

About two-thirds of the way through the movie, we witness Riley's imaginary best friend Bing Bong lose his imaginary rocket ship. He is devastated, believing that the rocket ship was the last piece of Riley he could keep, now that she feels too old to play with him.

The character named Joy insists on moving quickly to the next thing. There is urgency in the task at hand. She believes they do not have a moment to lose. But the character named Sadness sees a chance to sit and reflect. She waits at Bing Bong's side while he cries, making small remarks along the lines of: "I bet that feels really sad," and "It sounds like you really loved your time together."

After a few moments, Bing Bong is still weeping. And yet through the brief offering of intention, stillness, and active listening, he stands. Joy is stunned, asking of Sadness, "How did you do that?"

While she wasn't wrong, Joy's timing was off. There is always a possibility for joy to resurrect our broken moments, but allowing our heartaches to breathe means we will experience the same and have the strength to stand when we're ready to move again. Active listening is not dismissive, judgmental or directive.

Dismissive — "Don't worry."
Judgmental — "That can't be true."
Directive — "You should..."

Active listening does not require a resolution or an outcome. It requires a willingness to relinquish control over a circumstance, as well as your ability to influence the outcome. When active listening goes poorly, it usually results in inauthentic reframing.

Reframing

This is where the toxic positivity really shines like the broken prism that it is. Toxic positivity is a dark cloud over what should be a beacon of hope and promise. When taught by professionals, reframing is an incredible tool for mindset work. However, it can also be used casually with the goal of moving on quickly through the introduction of a snappy, pithy phrase meant to distract or inspire. The true premise is beginning to see your situation from another perspective, ideally coming to a more hopeful conclusion or course of action. Reframing is introduced within the timing of the person with the issue, not when those in support feel ready to encourage. Again, this is a matter of allowing discomfort with a circumstance to remain. Sometimes our thoughts become shaken and disorganized, and it will help to offer a grounding thought.

Reframing is a way that we can alter our perceptions of loss, stress, or life in general. It can create a more positive understanding of our circumstances and grief without making any physical changes. It can help and just as easily, be misused.

What we want to identify in reframing are the thinking patterns that cause our stressors in grief to amplify. Once they are noticed and allowed to breathe, we can move into challenging those thoughts with simple changes to our word choice. This becomes our personal practice over time. Attempting to reframe the thoughts of another person in the middle of their crisis will lead to mistrust. It is unlikely that someone will receive your positive reframing, even though they want to feel better. Feeling better doesn't come from ignoring how you feel. Reframing is not offering a distraction, minimizing the pain, or hijacking the attention.

Distraction — "Let's get a drink!"
Minimizing — "At least…"
Hijacking — "I know exactly how you feel. One time…"

Reframing is a technique for emotional wellness that we can use once a person is ready to experience their losses from another perspective. But turning every one of life's difficulties into a mantra for happiness is how we started stuffing our grief in the first place.

Once we can recognize toxic positivity, how do we avoid being hit when a well-intentioned archer takes aim with their good vibes? Most people mean no harm, so it's okay to lower your own weapons and defenses. Still, we can gently correct the comments that are not helpful while honoring our needs and the heart of the person speaking.

When a person is uncomfortable, they will do almost anything to avoid feeling awkward. So feel free to make it awkward — tell them to be quiet. By simply asking them to stop talking and sit with you, you are asking them to also feel. It's hard and necessary. "Can you just sit quietly with me, please?" If they cannot, you will know right away. Make a mental note that this person is not your inner circle when sorrow surfaces. That's okay; more on boundaries to come!

Another way we can manage inappropriate reframing is by being clear in response. It is your right to say, "Actually, that's not how I feel." Correct the assumptions but do not feel obligated to start a debate or change anyone's mind. Relating is a way we deepen our connections, but if they're built on a false premise, what then of the connection? By clarifying how our emotions are not bad, but information, we are embracing our own grief in a new way. We believe and accept that this loss is real, and that we will overcome each challenge as we continue to heal.

Tell Your Story

If you are in the state of mind to share, then share. When a person has handled your request for silence and the true declaration of what you feel, then the window is open. This is a person who can handle hearing you and holding space for you. Speaking and sharing your story is life-giving; **storytelling is a change agent.** As you speak, you will uncover things that reframe your thoughts even as the words leave your mouth. This is victory over toxic positivity; this is foundational revelation for when you truly are ready to move forward with yourself (not on or away from the problem).

None of these steps are about raising our own bow and starting a war. This is simply a nonviolent way of identifying what we need and learning how to ask for it. Toxic positivity assumes we all need the same thing — good vibes and high smiles. But we don't even know what we need right away, especially when things are difficult and the loss is fresh.

Learn to hear and appreciate your own voice. The initial framework of your crisis may be adding to the big emotions, but telling your story allows you to see yourself from another light. You're not pretending everything is wonderful. You are hearing yourself and giving yourself the benefit of the doubt instead of repeating the dismissive mantras. Allow the "yet" of growth to show up on your behalf.

Eight
The Yet of
Grief, Growth, and Healing

"Yet" is a mindset of expectation. When we are actively working through loss, we eventually come to know that while the pain is serious, it does lessen with time and intention. One of the most important ways we can honor our "yet" and protect our healing process is by understanding how to establish and maintain healthy boundaries.

Healthy boundaries guide our decisions and healing along the path we want to take. Unhealthy boundaries can derail our progress through a lack of focus or worse, by minimizing and dismissing our pain in the first place. If the idea of setting firm or new boundaries is terrifying, you're not alone. Although the steps can be overwhelming, learning to set boundaries for yourself in the grieving process invites your "yet" to the forefront. When you feel safe enough to open up within your community, vulnerability becomes the intention and healing the outcome. With careful intention, our inner work and expansion can establish boundaries that are long term, easy to remember, and even easier to recall and enforce.

New Boundaries

It is necessary to realize who can and who cannot hold space for you as you grieve. But doing so can feel like another form of grief in and of itself. Maybe someone you expected to remain steady cannot handle the ups and downs of your emotions right now. That doesn't mean they're no longer friends. But it may mean some intentional space is needed in this season.

When we make these big decisions to rework our inner circles, we may feel guilty. We are humans, wired for connection. It feels unnatural to reject a connection you typically enjoy. But you deserve to define who, why, and how others support you in grief, free of the burden to satisfy the expectations of others. Just because someone expects you to need them does not mean you are obligated to their presence. Healing without condemnation allows for true restoration. It may be time for you to shift the people around you, despite the potential for conflict. This is growth; this is grief — intertwined like the hands of lovers.

How can you tell if your circle is placing expectations on you as you try to heal? Earlier in this work, we discussed evaluating and setting new lines for our circle of support when we find ourselves hurting or frustrated. The following is an expanded discussion on how to identify the people in your circle of influence who are ready to be released.

One: You find yourself constantly justifying why their advice does not apply.

With the best of intentions, our loved ones often give us direction or ideas they truly believe will lessen our pain or shore up our grief. They start to "should" on us, making sure we know they have advice and experience that we lack. One client expressed a family member imploring him to move after losing his spouse. He could not fathom the idea, while other clients have moved almost immediately. For some, this advice could be helpful while for others, it may deepen the loss of connection to the person they lost. Either way, if you are deflecting their advice on a regular basis, they may not be the right fit for your support circle at this time.

Two: You find yourself consoling them over your loss.

Grief hijacking is a type of violent communication that goes unnoticed. It masquerades as empathy and active listening, but in reality the person is listening only long enough to hear how your story can relate to their own. Perhaps they only mentioned their miscarriage so you can feel less isolated in your grief. But regardless of intent, the outcome is the same. You find yourself now obligated to console the person who "showed up for you." If you've related by sharing a personal story while supporting another person, please know this is not a condemnation. In those moments, simply apologize and change course. But grievers must know they do not have an obligation to hold court and comfort for those unable to simply listen. We owe our stories to no one.

Three: You find yourself panicking at the thought of contact with them and consistently cancel plans or ignore their text messages.

This is pretty telling, yet incredibly difficult to admit. Recognizing how anxious you become at the thought of another coffee date or Zoom call with certain people is a warning. Anxiety rises quickly because your body is screaming for a change. While grief often leads to a season of detachment from the normal flow of life and its obligations, this is more specific to an individual rather than a responsibility. Avoiding volunteer roles or group gatherings makes sense; avoiding one person means something needs to shift with that one person.

The goal here? **To find yourself.** In the aftermath of loss, we also lose a sense of self that we may only notice when it feels too late. It isn't too late — but it may be harder to recover if you allow yourself to be surrounded in grief by those who inadvertently compound your pain. Finding yourself means finding the edges of what you will tolerate and establishing kind boundaries in a way that benefits you (the griever) first. You must put your stakes in the ground and maintain the space you need to honor your process of becoming.

I know confrontation is scary. But what if you reframe this boundary setting as an invitation? Setting clear, honest, and direct expectations for a friendship is incredibly kind. If the person reacts poorly, take that as a sign that the boundary might be more like a closing door, and that's okay. If the person decides to ghost you, then despite the passivity, the problem is resolved (for now). Just like children love to know how far they can go and remain safe, we deserve the same parameters for our healthy relationships to flourish and for our grief to reseed into growth.

Adjust The Existing Circle

There is a beautiful quote from adoption advocate and recording artist Ferara Swan:

"As we begin to heal a little more, we begin to tolerate a little less when it comes to how we deserve to be treated. Some may dislike that you're growing; others will love you more for it. Those are your true friends."

The moment you decide to set a boundary is the same moment you start figuring out who you want in your new circle, and how to keep it small.

One: Ask yourself, "What kind of person do I want in my circle?"

This is how you can refine your many connections into a trusted few that will gather around you in the lowest moments. If you are struggling to identify who those few may be, use your journal and write the characteristics of people who you can trust to hold space for you without judgment, correction, direction, or interruption. Your circle won't place demands on you to grow, heal, change, or fit their expectations while you are working through your pain. As you define the important characteristics, start to think of people you already know who fit those traits.

Two: Invite two or three of the people you've identified into an intentional relationship. You might say something like, "I'm in need of a trusted few who can draw closer and show up for me the way I need. Are you able to support me in this way?"

Be vulnerable. You're asking them to see you for who you are, where you are. It cannot be curated. You will benefit from authentically sharing what you need and what they can do to support you. If the person can't handle being in this type of a support system for you, that's okay. But if they say yes, then let them see you as you are. Allow them in.

Three: Ask them to help you clarify so they can actually offer support. "Do you understand what I'm asking of you?"

These aren't going to be strangers. Most of the time, these are people who already know you are grieving and have some idea as to why. Now, clarify. Invite them to ask you questions. Maybe you need clarity as well! Do you need someone to call when insomnia keeps you awake? Maybe you just need a silent walking partner, or a friend to text who won't respond with advice. The entire premise of a small circle is creating support you can trust when the difficult moments come.

You deserve this. It may not be simple, easy, or painless. But if something in life fits that bill, I haven't found it yet. Leaning into the discomfort of growth, even as we grieve, will allow us to reach the depths of our sorrow and to know we are not alone at the bottom. Become curious. Find the few who will feel your feelings with you, unafraid of catching your grief or losing their good vibes. You're worth it.

Who Do I Need or Want?

In the first days of a loss, it is human nature for so many to begin offering support. Everyone says, "Please let me know what you need." This is not helpful, as you often do not have a clue what you need. Maybe you don't want everyone to suddenly show up with a casserole or ask how you're handling the change.

Instead of inviting everyone who offers into your vulnerable moments, you have the privilege of designating a few key people for specific roles in your grief story. Rather than make space for everyone, you can call the circle closer and limit access for those who remain. This is crucial.

When you are establishing the circles, remember that you reserve the right to adjust as you go. You have permission to shift; to have needs that change as time goes on. You owe no part of your grief process to anyone around you (including the person you lost).

You may find it uncomfortable to set boundaries for those who no longer serve your healing as well as you would like. That's okay. This is a chance to practice honor for your own life and needs. Even as we grieve, we are learning to honor our process of becoming.

The type of people you find helpful in grief will differ, based on what you need or who you are. If you're still not sure, I have defined three roles below to seek out. Each role is a great starting point for grievers to begin finding their way back to a sense of influence and engagement with their own life.

Grief is an experience we do not ask for, but we can regain our independence bit by bit, starting with rebuilding the circle of people around us.

The Strong Back

This is the person who runs interference between you and the rest of the world. They're not afraid of confrontation or speaking on your behalf with your permission. This is the person who steps in when you need a strong back to support you and to confront you when your grief becomes overwhelming. Keep this person close; this is someone to whom you have nothing to prove. They can handle your rejection, your anger, and your heaviest emotions with grace because they know you need to get it out. This person is so safe for you.

The Soft Front

This is the person who immediately set up your meal train or delivered dinner. It should be someone you are close with, who you would trust to ask questions you'll forget: Food preferences, allergies, and more. They know when to stop talking. This is someone to whom you can articulate your direct needs without having to justify yourself. Your anger and changing needs will not damage this person because they're showing up out of love for you, not an obligation to serve in the time of need.

The Wild Heart

This is the person who you LOVE receiving text messages from. They're not loaded with platitudes or scriptures or memes; they're not trying to make you feel anything but loved. This is the person you can ask to schedule daily or weekly text messages or phone calls. This is someone who will hold space for you by remaining curious, patient, and compassionate. This is also someone who will remind you that you belong to yourself first. It is okay if you push back, hurt feelings *unintentionally*, or need space from the onslaught of supporters. This person will help you find yourself again as you feel deeply and heal slowly.

Clear Invitations

Learning to set boundaries is a lifelong skill, but as you invite the few trusted people into your inner circle, it is not a time to mince words. This is a season to be direct with your intentions and requests, as best as you can. Can you identify the three type of people listed above? If you feel that one of these roles is already filled, fantastic! If you realize the people in those positions need to shift, or you don't have someone in that role, today is the day to start thinking about who could show up for you.

Consider yourself an entrepreneur. All your friends want to work at your new company. They believe in you and your vision for the future. That does not mean that every one of them is the right fit for each role. The same is true in grief – our people want to champion our healing. We just can't hire everyone.

As you identify each individual, reach out face to face (if possible). Invite them into your "company" by clarifying how they've supported you and which role you need help with. Know this is a person where you can find vulnerability in their story as well – trust goes both ways, but it's okay to be the one that needs more as you heal. Ideally these supportive friends will remain close and connected throughout healing and beyond.

Setting and Upholding Healthy Boundaries

Remember, we don't want others to "should" upon us with their ideas about what is best in grief. Boundaries are about what we will tolerate, what we will not tolerate, and what we will do if our expectations are dismissed.

You are worth these boundaries. I've said it before, and I will say it to every person I work with for the rest of my life. You are worthy of love, respect, and all the time it takes to heal - even if that means keeping some people or behaviors at a distance.

We set these healthy, growth-minded boundaries by defining what we will accept, tolerate, and dismiss in our lives. As a griever, this will look a little different than traditional boundary work, but only barely. This is your chance to establish a baseline of what it looks like to support you as you heal. Take time to uncover what you want in a support system. Do you care if people call you at all hours? What does it mean "to support" your healing? It means something different to everyone. If you are willing to accept text messages, but will tolerate a weekly phone call from one specific person, then make sure you can actually enforce the boundaries you want to establish.

You also need to define your limits. Are you unwilling to tolerate platitudes in conversation? Make that clear. Do you want to avoid anyone stopping by unannounced? As we establish boundaries, it is our responsibility to communicate our expectations around them. But what if you share your expectations and someone drops by anyway?

Setting a consequence may feel punitive or unnecessary, but it is the best way to protect your healing process and make clear how serious you are about the boundaries you have set for your life. We've discussed how grievers can become passive to avoid "rocking the boat" or creating further discord in their lives, but if someone deliberately ignores your request, then they are not someone who can help you heal - no matter how much love or lasagna they provide.

When someone breaches our boundaries, we are emotionally triggered! It would be easy to justify passivity here, and it is always worth choosing your battles carefully. But your emotions are valuable, and to ignore enforcing your boundary to keep the waters still is unloving toward yourself. If you've communicated the boundary, then enforce your consequence when it's broken.

Maybe this looks like enforcing a "no platitude" rule. A boundary and consequence could sound like this: "If you continue to speak in platitudes when I've asked you simply to listen, then I am going to hang up the phone." It is crucial that the consequences are clearly communicated before you suddenly enforce them. This is how we honor our own limits and the person we want to redirect.

It would also be helpful to include your "strong back" person in these moments. Your boundaries require your reinforcement, but sometimes, grievers just don't have the energy. Have you ever just stopped responding to someone because of the amount of time and energy it takes? Grievers are often in these circumstances. Simply stop answering the phone. It would be easy to say that others are draining you, but it is up to you to define, uphold, and maintain your healthy boundaries. So if you are weary and unable to remove someone from your life in this season, allow another person to help you remain accountable to yourself and your healing.

A Quick Note on Codependency

When you engage in the work of healing, one of the "side effects" is awareness. You may begin to notice people around you exhibiting behaviors or expressing thought patterns we've addressed in this book. It's the gift of sight - once you notice you are healing, you start to notice healing (or opportunities) in other people. But we must guard against the tendency to push healing for someone else as much as we uphold our own boundaries.

Dependency is healthy in a relationship – both parties rely on one another for connection and to feel loved, valued, and supported without expectation. Codependency can trigger drastic emotional explosions when the gratitude is not reciprocated. A codependent person may define themselves by their connection to their enabler, feeling valued to an extreme. They may carry little ability to express themselves, their needs, or their perspective because all of that comes from the enabler. Sometimes the bereaved can inadvertently create these relationships. Usually this relationship already exists in your story, and your new loss will intensify the connection. The pain of codependency is amplified to eleven in grief, because your capacity is much lower than usual.

Codependency from others toward you looks (and may feel) helpful. But the dysfunction of it manifests significantly when you set a boundary and ask that person for space, or to stop attempting to help/fix your situation. It stops feeling helpful when you notice the other person is becoming attached, unable to accept your rejection of assistance, or becomes angry with you when you ask for space. Think of the last time you asked someone to stop sharing platitudes. How did they react? If you're dealing with someone struggling with codependency, the reaction may have looked like anger, accusation, or helplessness. "What am I supposed to do now?"

There are wonderful resources in the world about identifying and healing codependency, and I am not an attachment expert so this book will not go no further on the topic. But knowing how to recognize this unhealthy behavior will allow you to hold firm on your boundaries without counting yourself as mean, dismissive, rude, or out of line. Upholding your boundaries is loving behavior for both parties.

As a griever, you will slowly need less from the people who supported you in the beginning. Fewer people knocking and texting can be a relief! But as you need less, perhaps a few of the supporters will need to continue supporting your perceived needs, especially if they've been doing so in the past.

It will be tempting to allow the offerings to continue after your needs have changed. Even though you are in crisis, so is the person acting with codependent behaviors. It is an unhealthy pattern of life, but our role as receivers is not to take advantage of another's fluid or nonexistent boundaries. As we heal, both our methods of supporting others and supporting ourselves take new shape. If you are concerned that someone's support of you is to their own detriment, it may be worthwhile to step away from the relationship while you continue to heal. You can also ask for help from a third party to redefine the boundary you feel has been crossed.

Finding Your Breath and Voice

Our tendency in grief is to remain strong for everyone around us, but the truth is, without our own practice taking priority, what kind of strength can we truly offer another? We have a sense of duty and authority in the face of loss that leads us to believe that we must remain strong for everyone else. We must find the safety and freedom to fall apart.

The following excerpt comes from Mirabai Starr, a contemplative mystic and writer, on the sudden loss of her teenage daughter. Despite all her work cultivating a life of joy through multiple losses, the unexpected death of her child was "an avalanche annihilating everything in its path." In her own loss and experience, she goes on to describe the necessary time away to rediscover her ability to breathe.

"Suddenly, the sacred fire I had been chasing all my life engulfed me. I was plunged into the abyss, instantaneously dropped into the vast stillness and pulsing silence at which all my favorite mystics hint. So shattered I could not see my own hand in front of my face, I was suspended in the invisible arms of a Love I had only dreamed of.

Immolated, I found myself resting in fire. Drowning, I surrendered, and discovered I could breathe underwater."

We must recover our own oxygen first. Learning how to care for our heart; discovering what we need, what we don't need, and how to best implement the things that bring healing is something you can only understand from firsthand knowledge. I'm not suggesting that only those who have lost someone can relate or help in your healing, but experience is an incredible teacher. Our head knowledge gets us far enough, but refinement comes from the act of engaging our hearts.

Toni Morrison said, "The function of freedom is to free someone else." If we intend to find the freedom to exhale again through our healing, we must do it for ourselves. Our intention cannot be to learn how to grieve on behalf of someone else. I know well the desire to be strong for our friends and family. But no one can grieve for us, just as we cannot grieve for anyone else. No one else is experiencing our loss in the same way even if we lost the same person. The relationship, the nuance, and our connection needs its own time to be carried differently now that we are hurting. If we are not willing to let others do the same, both will suffer for our well intentioned actions of "trying to help."

Holding Space for Ourselves

Starting with ourselves feels selfish when we are used to being available. Showing up with casseroles and comfort blankets is what we do for others; is that what we should do for ourselves? It depends. The first step to learning how to hold space for your grief is to believe that you are worth the investment of time in your own life. Do you believe that your grief matters? If your answer is yes, then carry on. But if (for even a moment) you hesitate and attempt to minimize your own loss, then moving forward demands that you first remain still. Learning to sit with ourselves takes time, practice, and love for who we are. It requires us to believe we are valuable, no matter our current state of emotions or functionality. I am still valuable and worthy of love, attention, and healing – even when I haven't washed the dishes or contributed at church. You are inherently worthy of the time needed to work through your complex humanity and emotions. In order to heal, we must treat ourselves with the same gentle affection we would offer anyone else dealing with loss.

Your own heart cannot carry enough to heal those around you if it is walking with a limp. This is the whole point of this body of work; to find the tools and methods that help us manage our own grief first. Once you find some methods that reconnect you to your heart, invest the time it takes to do so. Reconnecting is not for the faint. It will feel gross, frustrating, slow, and confusing. But it will also feel triumphant, loving, and hopeful! The complexity of grief is going to manifest through the complexity of your humanity. You have emotions and you deserve the fullness of everything it takes to work through each one.

A friend recently expressed how in the wake of grief, someone told her she "shouldn't be sad to have lost the person because they would want her to be happy." The minimizing of her grief and emotions is just one of hundreds of examples of how not to hold space for another. As you consider how you want others to hold space for you, ask yourself, "What would I be doing for myself? How can I show up for my own heart right now?"

You know yourself better than anyone else. If hearing some encouraging scriptures would help you, then ask someone directly for that level of help. If hearing scriptures would make you want to jam your thumbs into your eyeballs, be honest about that, too. The intensity of grief does not mean you are beholden to carry another's response to your sorrow. Allowing false comforts to infiltrate your process as you're trying to heal is like eating healthy food you know has gone sour. What value are once fresh vegetables if they're decomposing? Compost!

You have a right to protect your space and your heart from the onslaught of support. Be selective – refer to the list of people who can be trusted and allow them to run interference if needed. And in the same way, be mindful that grief is not a permission slip to respond wildly and damage another. People are more likely to respond well and respect your words if you deliver it with gentle, loving kindness – even rebukes.

Boundaries, Tears, and Disenfranchisement

Instead of making dismissive comments like, "I don't have time to cry," what would it mean if you started to take up space for your process? Our lives are a whirlwind. On the best of days, we can focus on slowing down and rejecting the hurry. We can embrace a sauntering pace of love and invite peace into our present.

But even when we are not overwhelmed by the busyness of our days, it is rare to feel settled enough to cry. I'm writing about the privilege of setting boundaries, making time to mourn, and the freedom to embrace our grief. Humanity deserves equal access to loss accommodation. Even as I wrote the section above, my heart was heavy with the understanding that not everyone can safely implement and enforce an emotional boundary, let alone a physical one.

The privilege of crying is not something we talk about often, but then again, neither is grief. Have you ever scheduled a time to cry? How about taking a day off work simply because your loss is overtaking your focus? Maybe you're a CEO traveling 35 hours a week, but you haven't figured out how to feel comfortable sobbing on an airplane. Maybe you're a single parent, and it's easier to ignore your grief because the kids need your attention and a crying Daddy is not what you want to offer.

The privilege of grieving is also stigmatized. We are reminded almost daily to, "Get over it." There is a pervasive undercurrent in culture that disenfranchises our losses because they are expected, natural, or anticipated (such as losing an elderly family member). How often do you feel the pressure to hide your sorrow to protect the "good vibes" of the others?

It is natural to minimize our pain for the sake of self-comfort or to put others first. We are not less important, but have an internal propensity to place our emotional selves in a hierarchy of need. It's easy to say that a crying baby has more immediate needs than a grieving caregiver. While we can value putting the wellbeing of others first, we cannot do so at the sake of deepening our own wounds. Others do not deserve to grieve more than we do - comparing our losses to those who have "lost more" steals our self-awareness. We too are hurting. We too deserve to heal.

When others minimize our pain for their own benefit via platitudes, we push back. Discomfort is frequently seen as unacceptable, and because we are not used to holding ourselves as important, we submit to the cultural norm of grieving quickly and appearing "fine."

But just because these are natural reactions in our culture does not mean we must continue to honor them. Disenfranchised, ambiguous grief is everywhere. Ambiguous losses, such as a friendship that fell apart or a missed opportunity, are painful! The longer we allow these losses to be minimized and dismissed, the longer we will naturally struggle to process death in all its forms. Loss is loss. But to validate the emotional pain of another means doing the same for ourselves. If we choose to embrace loss in our own story, then we are starting the process of doing the same for others. If we are in a position to offer grace to someone in their grief, then we as humans must do so.

Are we the grieving CEO with single parents in our employ? Then as we gain our own awareness, we will see the value in making space and bereavement pay a core value of our company.

Are we the grieving parent? Then as we take a few minutes each day to check in with our heart, mind, body, and soul, our children will learn the value of honoring themselves, no matter how they feel.

In faith traditions, there is great emphasis on embracing our weaknesses. In a culture that glorifies the "Strong Man," the "Boss Woman," and the "Overly Mature Child Prodigy," we must work to reclaim the value of a tender heart. Having access to our emotional, intuitive side is not a weakness. Recognizing our shortcomings and inability to work 75 hours a week is wisdom. We gain strength through rest; by releasing our white-knuckle grips on life. And as we practice this release, we are living openhanded. This validates the revelations in loss that we cannot control this life or what happens to us.

We control our responses; our reactions and our beliefs. This is true strength — learning to bend and not break. Becoming flexible in our grasp on the physical life brings restoration to the innermost recesses of our spirit. We become internally indomitable where healing continues for a lifetime.

Learning to cry is another skill often left underdeveloped. The tender heart within us was created with a purpose! Tears are the body's method of clearing away what needs to be released. While our body releases tears to keep our eyes healthy and as a reflex response to irritants like wind, emotional tears contain higher levels of stress hormones when they leave the body. They literally purge our bodies of toxins. Endorphins are released when we engage our emotions and cry, decreasing physical pain and allowing an expression of the soul when we cannot find the words to speak.

Even if we believe we have permission to cry, finding the capacity to do so is complicated. Understanding your "Window of Tolerance" (as discussed previously) is one way to observe your own mental space and determine if you need some room to breathe.

The National Institute for the Clinical Application of Behavioral Medicine (NICABM) deals with clients experiencing trauma to help them cope with stressors and triggers. With each grief experience, our Window of Tolerance can narrow. Becoming aware of the stressors allows us to know when we have a greater capacity to process our tears. Essentially, when we are under duress, we can move into a place of hypoarousal or hyperarousal. Recognizing these states allows us to observe ourselves with the gift of nonjudgmental curiosity, which is a primary goal of restorative grief.

Hypoarousal is a state where we feel zoned out and disconnected from ourselves. A frozen numbness takes over our mental space and our capacity to process. Essentially, we shut down. Hyperarousal is the anxious, angry, reactive fight or flight response. Each of these is an innate self-protective response. They're not good or bad; emotions are information. Like the rest of our emotions, these states of being inform us of what we're encountering and provide a path to restoration as we carefully explore our stories with patience and compassion.

It is a great privilege to have the time to engage any of these concepts. While we may not have been raised to appreciate or value the emotional space in life, it is never too late to lean into vulnerability for our healing. However, it is a matter of access. The concept of vulnerability is becoming more and more prominent in our daily language, but not all people have an opportunity to learn how vulnerability can benefit the almost constant states of hyper or hypoarousal.

Grievers deserve to know their vulnerability will be championed and honored, but this only happens if we can champion and honor our own process first. No matter your role in life, you are worthy of healing. We may not all have experienced equal access to resources in our past, but as we lean into vulnerable conversations, despite the initial discomfort, we will invite others to do the same. We can create access for future generations by engaging our grief now. Whether our vulnerability is as visible as crying on a plane, or as intimate as confessing your sorrows to a friend, we are building atmospheres of grace where imperfections, tears, and growth are celebrated. We are creating literacy around grief and loss. We are creating a world where all are invited and welcome to heal.

Holding Space for Others - Yet in Action

Maya Angelou said, "As soon as healing takes place, go out and heal someone else." Healing in grief is a little like when you watch a new movie and cannot wait to talk about it with a friend. When we encounter knowledge that our spirit knows to be true, we rush into the world and declare it from the rooftops. Now that you are experiencing some movement in your process, you may think it's time for you to start explaining what worked for you in hopes that it will work for them, too.

But simply put, as you dash forward with your honest and available support, consider your own space and how you want to be heard in grief. Everyone needs their own time for "yet." Without our own moment of paused intention, your revelation and growth may seem little more than another platitude. We need space to heal for as long as it takes. The books, techniques, and tools you found meaningful may fall flat for another. Think back. What was one thing you truly wanted when you started to notice your grief?

In my experience, I wanted someone to remain with me, offering nothing but company. No expectations that I would share or heal. I could cry, speak, or simply press play for another rerun. Learning to hold space for others is a gift. Whether or not we are healing from our own losses, anyone reading this work is likely to be one full of empathy and compassion for others as well. Your desire to heal another is admirable, but requires more than a checklist. Healing is an individual process. If you are a grief-adjacent empathy warrior hoping to heal the world, give yourself a chance to instead offer support to just one person. Learn what they need, what they want, and show up authentically without trying to change the world all at once. Impact the world of one by helping them find a moment of "yet."

In your supporting role to grievers, there is always a chance you are serving from a position of obligation. Before you push back and defend your actions, pause to consider. Maybe you were raised in a culture requiring service to others as a mandate of your faith or community expectations. There is nothing wrong with the beliefs of community service and generosity – quite the opposite. The problem is that the same methods of caring for our neighbors do not easily translate into helpful support for those in grief.

It is easy to show up for a friend in a good mood with great news to share, and to listen with enthusiasm. It is exponentially more difficult to sit with those in trauma and remain patient, quiet, and attentive. No doubt you are reading this as you've suffered your own losses and know the importance of continuing to refine our hearts toward others.

Our intention cannot be to learn how to grieve on behalf of someone else. I know the pull of wanting to be strong for our friends and family. But the lifeline only holds when one end is secure. In the same way no one can grieve for us; we cannot grieve for anyone else. Despite any common ground, including sharing the person who died, we are unique in our grief and process. The relationships, the nuance, and the connection we carried need time to be carried differently now that we are hurting. If we are not willing to let others do the same, both will suffer for our well-intentioned actions of "trying to help."

Receiving Access

In the first interaction you have with someone who is actively grieving, please remember that clear, simple messages are kind and loving. It can be hard to remember what you needed in the initial days of your loss, especially when you've been working toward healing for a season. Honoring the loss of another means recognizing their boundaries, whether or not they've been communicated. Your newfound awareness means communicating that you will respect their needs, boundaries, and requests - even before they tell you what they need or want. Just say it – this is going to be a challenge, and I'm here for you if you'll have me.

But before you dive into offering your support, check your motives. Are you genuinely invested in their healing, or do you feel obligated to help? Resist inserting yourself into their story out of curiosity or a need to prove your own healing is real. When we are healing, we can become very strange versions of ourselves without noticing. Both you and your grieving friend will benefit from self-awareness.

Offering Resources

Think back again to when you first started to grieve. In the first few days or weeks, how many people offered resources you weren't ready to receive? Those of us experienced with grief are often quick to declare hope and growth from the lowest lows. However, it does not always serve others well to insist on finding hope in the beginning moments of grief.

As you are given access to the inner workings of someone else's loss, you will learn to serve with a new level of compassion. It is not our job to constantly encourage. It is our honor to hold quiet space and acknowledge the healing process. We bear witness to the story of another not by becoming a key player, but simply by allowing their story to unfold.

As a grief coach, I receive referrals for grief support on a weekly basis. We all know someone in grief. However, I find that most of the people referred to me are mere days into their loss. These grievers are nowhere near ready to work with someone action oriented, let alone start to heal. Survival mode, remember? The one thing grievers need in the first few days of loss is understanding and compassion, not referrals.

"When you're ready, I have plenty of resources. Until then, I'm available to listen and run whatever errands you need." This phrase, offered in earnest, is more supportive than you realize. Often, the simple act of establishing yourself as a resource is enough. They may not remember the name of the author you spoke about, but grievers will remember if you made them feel overwhelmed or settled.

Let's return once more to the first days of your own loss, but think about the people who showed up. Did you have someone you offered to simply sit quietly with you? This is the epitome of holding space. It is powerful to know your silence makes space for healing to step in. In the quiet, you can invite the presence of the comforter directly into the situation. There is nothing about holding space for someone in grief that requires you to be responsible for their process or their emotions. You are responsible to be the friend you promised you could be. You are responsible to show up.

When we go through the weird discomfort of trying to figure out how to help someone, we should also invite them to give us ideas about what they might need. Eventually, they'll learn how to ask for what they need. In the meantime, offer to show up with a pizza and a box of tissues. Or to be available for the middle of the night panic attacks as someone who can just listen to the overwhelm of the moment. I wish I'd felt safe calling someone in the middle of my insomnia. Not that I couldn't have called my family; I simply gave them the space I thought they also needed.

What would it mean to teach others they can take up space?

Do you remember how it felt to start asking for what you needed? Maybe it's time for you to remind grievers they have permission to ask for the same. Sometimes, this is the easiest gift you can offer: to remind a human their needs are valid. That the time it takes for them to heal is exactly how long it takes.

There is no comparison to the process of others, but we consistently forget to keep our eyes on ourselves when we see the health of another. Comparison and self-condemnation are easy habits to trip over; our role as support can be to remind the grievers how to love themselves with patience and compassion instead.

Epilogue

Grief literacy is a crucial part of our framework as humans. But in our hurry to find safety, security, and certainty, we may sacrifice growth and understanding for what we believe is comfort. We want control over our lives and the outcome. When we realize we have little to no true influence over the outcomes, we tend to become indignant and dismissive of whatever stands in our way. And when a loss highlights just how impermanent life is, we either settle into the discomfort or we double-down on indignation and dismissal. Learning how to navigate grief without minimizing our emotions, dismissing our grief, or comparing our losses to that of others - this is the work. This is the paradox: to willingly lean into our losses while remaining anchored firmly to a grounded sense of self. This is where we find peace with impermanence.

While much of this book is my personal experience with loss, there is so much here you can take as your own. I often receive questions as to why this is the path I chose. After all, so many of us have experienced a death that did not course correct our lives into working in this field.

While a career in grief is not glamorous, it is wildly necessary. I want to live in a world where we can know our losses will be honored — where a gentle word is offered as a reflex, over directives to "man up," or "get over it."

But grief is complex and nuanced. If we had an easy answer, the confusion would dissipate instantly. If we want to live in a world where emotions are honored, humanity is valued, and growth is embraced, then we must lean into creating work with a lasting impact for the generations behind us to champion and expand.

We do not exist in a vacuum. There are no straight lines from A to Z, nor are there black and white answers to healing through grief. The beauty of this uncomfortable reality is that we are free to find movement in our methods. We can be with others and feel alone – why then can we not be alone but feel embraced?

Working through grief with a mindset of growth and permission means constantly checking myself for the harmful thoughts around loss. Can I find movement and learn a new way of thinking about grief? Can I offer compassion without judgment to myself and others? These questions are constant, no matter where you find yourself in your healing process. Remaining (or becoming) curious about our own response to loss is the reminder we need to continue the work. It is a reminder that even when the pain is increasing and the hopelessness seems bigger than ever, we are not alone. The work of healing will always highlight the paradox of life, of faith. This is grief. Through practice, we can trust that even through the pain, there is joy to be found.

In the next pages, you will find a list of resources to guide you through the never ending healing process. And as much as I wish I could confirm a true end to grief exists, I can only confirm the opposite. The last thought I want to leave you with is that while you navigate loss in any form, please hold yourself in high regard. In seasons of great pain, it is easy to lose sight of who we are and what we believe. It is easy to believe we are not worth the work. Grief can be blinding; and so we do this work to regain sight and reorder our thoughts and lives around the loss.

Hold your heart, mind, body, and soul with gentle, loving hands as you go through every moment of grief. And when you feel you cannot possibly carry your heart any further, may you remember that you are not carrying it alone.

Resources

Books Referenced or Recommended

Rising Strong by Brene Brown

Braving the Wilderness by Brene Brown

Breathe by James Nestor

Boundaries for Self by Allison Cook, PH.D.

Connect by Teri Alison Murphy

Soul Rest by CZ Zackery

No Mud, No Lotus by Thich Nhat Hanh

Closure: The Rush to End Grief and What It Costs Us by Nancy Berns

Motherless Daughters by Hope Edelman

Trauma Stewardship by Laura van Dernoot Lipsky

Grieving Mindfully by Sameet M Kumar, PH.D.

Additional Support and Concepts Discussed

- Join The Restorative Grief Project on Facebook at
  https://www.facebook.com/groups/rests

- Window of Tolerance by Dr. Dan Siegel at
  https://www.nicabm.com/trauma-how-to-help-your-clients-understand-their-window-of-tolerance/

- The Dougy Center - Grief Support for Children & Families
  at https://www.dougy.org/

- Contemplative Outreach - Guided Prayer Work at
  https://www.contemplativeoutreach.org/

- Exploring the Examen Prayer at
  https://www.jesuits.org/spirituality/the-ignatian-examen/

- Modern Loss - Online Grief Community at
  https://www.modernloss.com

- Grief in Motion Podcast with Kristine Gunningham at
  https://www.instagram.com/griefinmotion/

- Identifying Cognitive Distortions at
  https://positivepsychology.com/cognitive-distortions/

- Breathing videos, expert advice and more at
  https://www.mrjamesnestor.com/breath-vids

Gratitude

I don't know where this book or my own heart would be without the brave people navigating my panic attacks, heartaches, and occasional imposter syndrome. My family has no idea how much grounding they've offered through this process!

Josh, my faithful and patient husband! You've held space with kindness through my biggest meltdowns and greatest triumphs. I'm quite sure I'll never find the words to thank you enough, but I'll continue to try with each breath.

Eleanor, you are a light in a world of darkness. Thank you for being the reminder of hope made manifest in a season of so many sorrows. I pray I continue to be the mom you wished for. I will always love you with my whole heart!

Samantha, you're only six years younger but wise beyond your years. Being your sister has made me a better woman, better mom, and better friend. I love your guts. You are every ounce as super as me and a champion I hardly deserve. I'm so grateful for you.

Dad, I love you more than words can ever say. To know you is to know the very embodiment of generosity and love. Thank you for being my champion, always.

Renee and Nana, I'm not sure losing Mom was survivable without the two of you. I'm so glad we're not alone.

To my girls - Alyssa, Ashley, and Rachael! I can't believe you have held me so close for so long. It is my great honor to share a table with you. Thank you for seeing me and loving me anyway!

Ryan, thank you for editing and spending so much time on this labor of love! I'm glad I didn't scare you off all those years ago. You probably should have run the other direction. I'm so grateful you didn't.

Kate, thank you for believing in me! Your willingness to champion my vision and carry me with prayerful intention through each season of this book reminded me to believe in the truth of who I am and why these words are necessary.

My goodness, I feel rich with names to include and could write a second book simply honoring the people who love me so intentionally. My chosen family is huge! So I'll finish with this: If you're reading this right now, then yes — your name is on that list!

About the Author

Mandy Capehart is a certified grief and life coach, and creator of The Restorative Grief Project. She co-hosts The Uncomfortable Grace Podcast, as well as leads Women's Fight Night, a nondenominational community of Christian women sharing stories of their faith and growth. Mandy currently lives in Southern Oregon with her husband, daughter, and Border collie rescue dog. She loves celebrating local winemakers and spending as much time outdoors as possible — with all the sunblock, of course.

The Restorative Grief Project is an online coaching community focusing on one another's stories and new methodologies for grief, creating a safe environment for our souls to heal and our spirits to be revived. To learn more, visit MandyCapehart.com.

Follow & engage Mandy on Twitter & Instagram: @MandyCapehart

Thank you for reading. May you find beauty in the tension between stillness and movement as you work your way toward wholeness.

Restorative Grief

Made in the USA
Las Vegas, NV
17 November 2021